...shed by Relevant Pages Press, Charleston, South Carolina.

www.relevantpagespressllc.com

Cover design by Owais Uz Zaman of 99 Designs,
https://99designs.com/

Interior Layout by Betts Keating Design,
www.bettskeatingdesign.com

ISBN-13: 978-1-947303-1-9

Printed in the United States of America.

COLLEGE
— IS NOT —
MANDATORY

**A Parent's Guide to Navigating the Options
Available to Our Kids After High School**

STEPHANIE R. HAYNES

Publi

TABLE OF CONTENTS

ACKNOWLEDGMENTS 7

INTRODUCTION 9

HOW TO USE THIS BOOK 13

A NOTE: PARENT TO PARENT 15

PART ONE: THE BACKGROUND 17
HOW THE "COLLEGE FOR ALL"
MENTALITY IS HURTING OUR KIDS 19

PART TWO: EXPLORING THE OPTIONS 31
THE BENEFITS OF THE LOCAL COMMUNITY
COLLEGE: THERE ARE MORE THAN YOU THINK ... 33
• COMMUNITY COLLEGE CASE STUDIES 41

LEARN A SKILL AND (POSSIBLY) GET PAID TO
DO IT: APPRENTICESHIP AND TRADE SCHOOL
PROGRAMS 51
• APPRENTICESHIP AND TRADE SCHOOLS
CASE STUDIES 63

JOINING THE MILITARY AFTER HIGH SCHOOL
HAS MORE BENEFITS THAN YOU THINK 81
• MILITARY CASE STUDIES 91

CAN A GAP SEASON BE BENEFICIAL? YES! 107
• GAP SEASON CASE STUDIES 115

WHEN COLLEGE IS RIGHT IT WORKS 131
• 4-YEAR COLLEGE CASE STUDIES 141
• COLLEGIATE ATHLETE CASE STUDIES 155

PART THREE: THE NEXT STEPS GUIDE 161
  NEXT STEPS STARTING POINT 163

  NO CLUE? NO PROBLEM! START HERE 173
    QUESTIONS: VALUES 179
    QUESTIONS: PASSION POINTS 181
    QUESTIONS: CAREER PATHWAYS 183

  PUTTING IT ALL TOGETHER 187
    HOW TO DETERMINE IF A COMMUNITY
    COLLEGE IS A GOOD FIT FOR YOU 191

    HOW TO DETERMINE IF A TRADE SCHOOL
    OR APPRENTICESHIP PROGRAM IS A GOOD
    FIT FOR YOU 197

    HOW TO DETERMINE IF THE MILITARY IS
    A GOOD FIT FOR YOU 203

    HOW TO DETERMINE IF A GAP SEASON IS
    A GOOD FIT FOR YOU 207

    HOW TO DETERMINE IF A 4-YEAR COLLEGE
    IS A GOOD FIT FOR YOU 211

    HOW TO DETERMINE IF BEING A COLLEGIATE
    ATHLETE IS A GOOD FIT FOR YOU 217

ENDNOTES 221

This book would not be possible without the influence, advice, and experience of so many others.

Thank you, first, to my husband and children who tolerated my constant discussions and questioning while I worked through the creation of this book. Your willingness to always support me fills my heart and gives me the confidence to reach for higher stars.

This book would not have come to life without the discussions, research, and dreaming with my friend and partner in parenting Jennifer Tubbiolo. Thank you for always pushing me out of my comfort zone.

To all who allowed me to interview them in order to build my knowledge about each of the options available to students after high school, thank you. Your efforts at producing multiple pathways to success for today's high school students is exemplary.

To those parents and students who completed the surveys I sent out for the case studies, thank you for your honesty. The readers of this book are blessed by your willingness to share your stories.

The idea for this book was born from the hundreds of conversations I've had with parents and students about developing a successful career pathway after high school. As an educator and professional Education Coach and Consultant, I've had many opportunities to hear and observe, first-hand, the struggles of parents and teens as they navigate the options available to them after high school. So many teenagers are overwhelmed by the magnitude of the decisions in front of them that they often shut down completely or, worse, simply follow what all their friends are doing. So many parents have stories of doing what they thought they were supposed to do in their own post-high school years only to "wake up" in the future with regret over their choices. These regrets now influence whether they feel capable of helping their teenagers make their own decisions.

WHY WE NEED THIS BOOK

High school counselors are fantastic at their jobs but are often overworked by the number of students on their caseloads. Individual Graduation Plan meetings[1] are often 20-30 minutes or less with little real reflection time or guidance to help students decide what to do after high school.

Student's approach to choosing their academic coursework has become focused on developing their competitiveness for collegiate acceptance or simply graduating high school rather than exploring potential career pathways. There are plenty of businesses focused on helping students plan and pay for college, but little amplification is given to choices aside from the 4-year college, though many opportunities exist.

As a high school teacher, I have worked with thousands of students who had no idea how to figure out what to do with their lives after high school. As an Education Coach and Consultant, I have seen a significant rise in the number of teenage clients (high school through college age) who are searching for someone to help them "figure their life out." All of these teenagers want to be successful and happy in life but have not had the time, the opportunity, or the training to explore their options, reflect on their values, identify their passions, and understand how to process all the options in front of them. They struggle with fear of missing out or messing up or not measuring up to the high expectations they've placed on themselves and so they become stuck.

Parents are becoming increasingly aware there are multiple options for their teenagers after high school, but don't know how to identify them or how to help their teen understand the benefits of each option available to them after high school. Additionally, after decades of societal pressures touting 4-year college degrees as the best predictor for future success, parents struggle with the "FOMO" mentality: will their teen miss out on something if they don't go to a 4-year college right after high school?

As I've worked with my students and teenage clients (and their parents) over the years I have come to develop a process:

1. Help them identify their values and passion points.

2. Guide them into a growth mindset about their future and the development of meaningful goals.

3. Work with them to identify all their potential career pathways and the options available to them.

4. Teach them how to research each option effectively and establish a post-high school pathway to personal success.

What I have come to realize is there are many more teens who need this kind of process than I can help individually, and so the idea for this book came to life.

HOW TO USE THIS BOOK

This book is not intended to promote any pathway as better than another. It is meant to provide the opportunity to explore the many options available to teenagers in a way that allows them to process and reflect on each option's benefits and drawbacks for themselves. I hope that because of working through this book, parents will be able to guide their teenagers in meaningful discussions that help them reflect on the relevance of each option to their values and goals in life.

Each chapter provides a general overview of each of five major options available to students after high school: Community Colleges, Trade Schools and Apprenticeship Programs, The Military, Gap Seasons, and 4-Year Colleges (including collegiate athletics). Each chapter has several case studies of student experience so teens might "see" themselves in that option, as well as parent interviews of what it was like from their perspective to help their teenager make the decision they did. Also included is a special Next Steps Guide that includes specific reflective questions and research options for parents to use in developing with their teen the best possible pathway to a meaningful future.

A NOTE PARENT TO PARENT

As one parent to another, I know how tough it is to help your teen when they are struggling. We all want to have the answer, we all want to help them make their decision. Often, they rely on our direction, but this is an area we should only serve as a guide, not the director. For our teenagers to truly be successful in life they need to own their own decisions about their future. Our job at this point is to help them identify their options (including their financial responsibilities within each option), act as a sounding board as they work out their thoughts, and support them as they make the decision they see as best for themselves, *whether or not we agree with their choice.* This is tough to do, I know, but it is essential for their growth and development into adulthood. We all want our teenagers to develop into responsible adults; helping them identify this next stage of their lives and allowing them to claim the rewards and experience the consequences is a great way to do this.

As parents, we may also need to do some work here. We need to identify what we're willing to accept and what we are willing to provide and make those expectations clear to our teenagers. For example, if we are willing to pay for college, trade school, or a gap season, what requirements, expectations, and deadlines are on that financial gift? Will we tolerate a teen living at home indefinitely? How long will we allow a high school graduate to wander with no plan? What are the consequences of not making a choice or even putting in the time to research options?

It is human nature to follow the path of least resistance. As parents we can help set up guardrails and guide our teenagers into a future that is successful for them, allowing them to make their own choices while setting up boundaries around our involvement. The result can be a plan teens are academically prepared for, emotionally prepared for, and financially prepared to step into after graduation.

May your experience using this book be blessed and fruitful!

PART ONE
THE BACKGROUND

HOW THE "COLLEGE FOR ALL" MENTALITY IS HURTING OUR KIDS

Getting a college degree has been hailed as the most valuable way for today's high school graduates to be successful in life. That's just not true and that lie is hurting our kids.

When I graduated high school in 1987 most of my classmates did not plan on attending a 4-year college. There was no pressure to go to college or pursue any other specific option for that matter. The mentality was to choose what worked best for us and our decision was based on what we wanted to do with our lives not what option was better. Our parents were hardly involved, though supportive. We all just seemed to choose the pathway that worked for us, without fear of not being good enough.

When I started teaching high school 5 years later, I noticed that among my students a subtle shift in perspective had occurred. The message now being spread to them

Here's the Main Idea

Over the past few decades, the mentality of success has been funneled into one success path, 4-year college, to the detriment of our kids.

was promoting college as a "savior" from the financial instability their parents had endured as well as representing the ability to earn a more prestigious career. The language in education became more fear-based; students would not be successful if they couldn't do better than their parents, and the only way actively promoted to do this was a college degree. Additionally, colleges, experiencing more and more students coming onto their campuses, started expressing frustration at the lack of preparedness of students, so the curriculum began shifting from skills-based to more liberal arts, college-prep based. By the time I moved from that school 10 years later, over 75% of students believed that a college degree was essential to their success in life.

When I returned to the classroom in 2017, 100% of my students believed they needed to get into a 4-year college to be successful. And, worse, it had become more than just getting in. Words like "bridged" or "wait-listed" somehow made a teen less than successful and big-name colleges had more "street cred" weight than others, further affecting a student's idea of success.

Parents and teachers had even gotten into the crazi-
ness, pushing students to excel in school at every grade
level, instilling the fear that if they didn't do well in school
now they wouldn't be able to get into college, which meant
they wouldn't be successful. The message to students: a
college degree is the only pathway to success in life and
if you don't measure up and qualify to get into the best
schools, you aren't good enough.

Over the past few decades, the mentality of success has
been funneled into one success path, 4-year college, to the
detriment of our kids.

WHY DOES THIS HURT OUR KIDS? HERE'S WHAT I HAVE SEEN

On average there is more anxiety among teenagers due to performance in school than ever
before. The National Education Association[2] published an article calling anxiety an "epidemic,"
stating that over 70% of teens say anxiety and
depression is a "major problem." Why? In my
experience as a high school teacher and Education Coach and Consultant, it comes mostly from
the pressure to succeed. Parents are pressuring
them, teachers are pressuring them, the "keeping
up with the Jones'" mentality is pressuring them
all to conform to one way of becoming successful.

☛   Over the past decades, an increasing number of school districts have shifted from a partial hands on learning approach (offering car repair courses for example) into more "collegiate worthy" liberal arts education elective courses. However, not every student is adept at school, nor do they have an interest or even passion for a liberal arts education. There is a whole population of teenagers being told they aren't good enough simply because they don't fit into the current schooling mold. These students often seem uninterested in school and do not live up to what their parents know they are capable of. Bored and uninterested they naturally act out or tune out and are erroneously labeled as trouble-makers, further reinforcing the message that they aren't good enough.

☛   From an incredibly young age, children are taught that college is their future with little discussion about how to achieve what they might want to do in different ways. Yet, there are hundreds of pathways to success. Certificate programs at the local community college or technical school, apprenticeship programs, transfer programs to reduce student debt, military options, and purpose-filled gap seasons can all lead to huge opportunities for students without the hefty price tag and years involved in something that doesn't suit them. Yet, to most teens and their parents, these options often feel less than prestigious compared to 4-year colleges and as if there was some standard that couldn't be met so they "settled" for a different option.

🎓 Many parents have become consumed with the college acceptance letter as a marker of their success. I have spoken with countless parents who fear their teen will not be successful if they don't have straight A's and don't get into "the" college for their area. The term "helicopter parent" causally relates to this mentality: parents hover over their teen to make sure they don't fail so that they can get into the right school and be successful. Parents can't seem to allow their teenagers to fail because it means they are a failure in their parenting, yet nothing could be further from the truth.

The problem with this mentality overall is that a college degree does not guarantee a successful life. Period. Brian Buffini, a parent of six and successful entrepreneur with no college degree (though his children are in college) says this about college[3]: "There's a lot of things that work in college that don't work in the real world, and I am more and more convinced all the time at how poorly college prepares young people for success."

What does guarantee success? An individual's passion to pursue greatness on their terms. Unfortunately, we are systematically drumming the opportunity for this out of our kids.

HOW ADULTS CAN HELP

It is up to all of us as parents (I have 2 children), extended family, teachers, career counselors, and even education policymakers to end the "college for all" mentality and instead help our teenagers learn about all of their options and equip them to choose the one, or combination of options, that's best for them.

This guidebook is meant to do just that. I believe there is no one route suited for all teens. There is, however, a pathway all teenagers can take to determine what next steps after high school will be most beneficial for them:

1. Identify their values.

2. Identify their passion points in life.

3. Determine a career cluster area that excites them based on their values and passions.

4. Develop a growth mindset to believe they can create a successful future for themselves.

5. Identify the best option, or combination of options, to pursue.

I have used this process with my children as well as hundreds of students in a classroom setting and as individual clients. When a teen engages in this process and is successful in identifying potential opportunities forward for themselves, they are freed from the fear and insecurity that holds them back. It's incredible to see how confident they become not only in themselves but in their ability to engage with their current education process in a meaningful way.

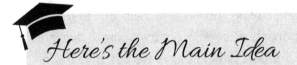

Here's the Main Idea

What does guarantee success? An individual's passion to pursue greatness on their terms. Unfortunately, we are systematically drumming the opportunity for this out of our kids.

Too often there is little to no guidance whatsoever to help teenagers make arguably one of the biggest decisions in their lives. Our society has chosen for them a single route that may not work for them, reinforcing the idea that they just aren't good enough if they can't succeed. I have heard from countless parents who watched their teenagers' self-esteem plummet (and arguing rise) year after year because they did not fit the traditional school-to-college route. These students need the opportunity and guidance to explore all the options available to them so they can discover one that fits them best. Continuing to limit everyone to the one-size-fits-all mentality leads to a heightened opportunity for today's teen to become so mired in negative mindsets they struggle for years to ever figure out what success truly means to them.

WHY IT'S IMPORTANT
TO EXPLORE ALL THE OPTIONS

There are so many options available today. One size does not fit all and taking the time to help our teens determine the best option or even a combination of available options is one of the best gifts I believe we can give them.

It is tough to consider other options. The cultural norm of college for all is strong and not pursuing that option still feels like somehow our kids might miss out. What I hope you will consider is what is most important: our children's ability to be successful in life according to their terms. Teenagers will struggle, no matter what option they choose. They will make mistakes, change course, and redirect. We did too. Our struggles, and our choices in how we handled those struggles, made us the people (and parents) we are today. I believe we need to allow our teens to experience the same. They are not us. They live in a different time than we did and have different personalities than we do. They will make choices different from ours and need to be allowed to do so. We need to give our teenagers the opportunity to wrestle with life, remembering that our struggles gave us the opportunities we needed to succeed and can do the same for our teens.

In September of 2020, I asked a private Facebook group of local moms the following question: What are your thoughts/beliefs about a 4-year college being the best option after high school? Their answers (over 188 of them) indicate clearly that there is a growing shift into considering the individual teenager over the cultural norm (responses have been edited for space):

> *Education is important and should be a lifelong pursuit, however, there are many forms of education other than pursuing college degrees. Our oldest daughter did a semester of college after graduation. It was a good experience for her, but she has chosen to leave and serve on a mission for 18 months. I'm sure she will have more thoughts and change of plans after she comes home from that.*

> *My husband and I are going to encourage our kids to join the Air Force after high school. I think going out into the real world a bit helps people figure out what they want to do.*

> *I think it depends on the child. I have four. One went to college on a football scholarship and is absolutely made for this, one went on a full-ride academic scholarship and dropped out to go to cosmetology school. One hated it and the fourth isn't there yet. I definitely think it 100% depends on the child and what they want.*

I think it's great for some and unrealistic for others. I'm not pushing my son to do that. He's highly intelligent, but school is difficult for him. I think, as parents, we should have open and honest conversations about this. No need to rush into a 4-year school or the debt that comes with it if they aren't ready!

High school teacher here. A four-year college degree is amazing for some, but not for all. I honestly believe education should fit the needs of the student and a 4-year degree is not for every student.

As a single mom who would be out of work without my college degree, I preached it! I preached it to my girls to get a degree to be able to always support themselves if anything bad happens. After dealing with the prices of schools, debt, and realizing a lot of people don't use their degree I started preaching trade! Get a trade, be honest, be on time do the right thing by your customers, etc. Either is good but with my third daughter, I'm preaching trade and save the student loan debt.

Depends on the kid. I think the whole going to college to find out what you want to do can be a huge financial drain and a waste of time. Everyone should follow their passion. Anyone who is motivated can be successful in the capacity that will make them happy.

I told my son only to go to school when you are ready and know exactly what you want. Even though it's been frustrating as a mom to watch him not progress as I see so many around him are, I haven't pressured him. I want him to craft his own life independent of what I want for him. I've realized that I'm no expert at happiness, so I should leave him to his own devices to figure out what is best for him.

All the options included in this book are equally valuable. I hope you will choose to focus on helping your high school student determine the pathway to success that matters most to them. We can choose to no longer accept the mentality that a 4-year college is the only route of success for all. It is time to help our teenagers break out of the mold, examine all the opportunities available to them, and guide them into making the decision that best suits them.

Our world needs more variety and less conformity. Imagine what our culture would be like if every teenager were encouraged and given guidance to explore all their options and given the freedom and support to choose what works best for them. Imagine how personal success on their terms could affect the disposition of our maturing teenagers. The investment of time to help our teens process and identify what works for them is well worth it. If that is a 4-year college degree right after high school, fantastic. If it is not, how much happier will our teens be for having had the opportunity to determine for themselves what fits them best. Isn't that what we are all after?

PART TWO
EXPLORING THE OPTIONS

THE BENEFITS OF THE LOCAL COMMUNITY COLLEGE: THERE ARE MORE THAN YOU THINK

Samuel's* parents approached me because they were worried about him. As a high school junior in his second semester, they did not believe he had the grades for a 4-year college. There was interest from college baseball coaches, but his parents believed he would not be able to receive an offer unless he got his grades up. Their relationship with Samuel was strained as a result.

In my initial conversation with Samuel, he shared his love for his sport as well as a desire to attend a 4-year college to be able to play. He wasn't sure what to do for a major and felt overwhelmed by trying to figure everything out. As a result, he admitted he struggled to do his school-work. He didn't believe he would be worth a coach's time to recruit because his grades were already "bad."

* not their real names

Over the next few sessions, Samuel and I processed his values and his passions and discovered that in addition to playing his sport he wanted to become a Paramedic. We researched the colleges he was interested in as well as the local community college EMT program. He discovered that this particular option gave him the ability to play his sport and earn an AA degree that could help him develop the grades to transfer to a 4-year college while also earning a certificate to earn a living as an EMT to support himself. The final benefit came when addressing the costs of all the options he was considering. The 4-year colleges weren't offering him any financial assistance other than loans (which he did not want), but the local community college offered free tuition, an offer to play his sport, and a way to earn money to pay his way through his final two years to earn a BS as a Paramedic.

The truth is that utilizing the benefits of the local community college may prove a better investment of time and money for some students than attending a 4-year college right after high school.

While a 4-year college degree has been proven to increase income, there are untold benefits for teens in utilizing the local community college as part of their plan for a successful future. Thousands of students do not fit the 4-year-college-right-after-high-school stereotype and yet there is pressure to apply to numerous universities, choose a somewhat interesting major, extend themselves into debt, and try to make it work.

Why? I propose it's because the mentality in our culture has become centered on success being determined solely by a college degree. But this just isn't true.

As many who have earned that college degree have learned, a college degree does not guarantee a well-paying job or even a career they are passionate about. Additionally, many start life tens of thousands of dollars in debt.

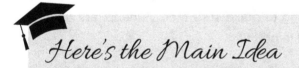

Here's the Main Idea

The truth is that utilizing the benefits of the local community college may prove a better investment of time and money for some students than attending a 4-year college right after high school.

While it is true that many careers do require a 4-year degree (or more) and a degree usually creates a stronger salary, what's not true is that there is only one pathway to get there. Many overlook one of the best options in front of them: The local community college.

The local community college offers a plethora of options for today's high school graduate. In fact, almost anything that can be accomplished at a 4-year university (aside from advanced degrees) or even a trade program can be accomplished at a community college.

Community colleges, like trade schools, must remain competitive in today's market of post-graduation options. They offer complete certification programs that provide necessary career development training as well as specific skill development, transfer programs, and Associate of Arts degrees, all for much less than a traditional 4-year college or some trade school programs. Like 4-year colleges, community colleges offer academic services and career planning and placement services in addition to traditional academic advising to make sure their students are getting where they want to go.

Unfortunately, many of the positive opportunities offered by today's community colleges are often overlooked. High school students and parents seem to see them as less prestigious and therefore less worthy of consideration. Additionally, attending a community college often means a teenager will continue living at home which, to most teens, can feel like their efforts at stepping into adulthood are being stymied.

Why should parents and students stop and consider this option before automatically moving into a 4-year college right after graduation? Here are some things to consider:

 Not every student does well in traditional school settings. Some teens thrive in the traditional model, but there is a growing number who do not. Specialty charter schools and home schooling are all seeing increases that indicate this. Community colleges offer a wide variety of specialty certificate programs that give teens the opportunity to learn valuable skills in a hands-on environment and earn well-paying jobs in less time than spending 4 or more years in a classroom.

 Some students are not ready to move away from home and live on their own. Many teens idealize living in a dorm and having complete freedom, but for some this can have devastating effects. Many high school graduates still struggle with time management, schoolwork organization, and being mature enough to handle the pressures they will face both physically and socially in college. Spending time at a community college right after high school can allow these students the time to develop stronger skills and mature. This extra time may even prevent them from failing out after their first semester (and losing thousands of dollars), protect them from getting overwhelmed and discouraged, and give them a better chance of succeeding in their coursework while building stronger self-confidence.

 Some students just are not sure what they want to study. Community colleges offer a way to earn a transferable Associate of Arts degree by getting all the general education require-ments completed. During that time, a student can research potential majors, career pathways, and even additional opportunities which can greatly help them narrow down their options. Why commit to a 4-year school only to change your major three times (which is the average amount of major change students experience) or even decide it's not worth it when you can spend two years, in the beginning, figuring it all out ahead of time?

Some community colleges offer free or reduced tuition. In California, as well as many other states in our nation, residents can attend community college for free or at greatly reduced costs. In South Carolina, lottery funds are applied to all SC residents to reduce tuition costs by almost half when attending as a full-time student. Traditionally, community colleges cost less than colleges and universities, potentially preventing our kids from starting their adult lives tens of thousands of dollars in debt.

According to a 2019 article on credit.com[4], these are the student debt facts:

- Average student loan debt total per person: $31,172

- Average monthly student loan payment for graduates: $393

- Total student loan debt in the U.S.: $1.52 trillion

- Time to pay off student debt: 10 to 30 years

On average, at least two full years of a 4-year college degree can be taken at a community college. Additionally, if you are a high school student who wishes to attend an out-of-state school (which dramatically increases costs) attending a local community college in that state can help you earn residency as well as give you transferable credits.

 Some students would benefit from playing their sport at this level. Playing a sport at the collegiate level is not an easy thing to do. Teens who wish to play their sport past high school may do very well starting at the community college level, building up their strength, endurance, and skill, making a name for themselves, and increasing their GPA. At that point, they may be better qualified and prepared to play at the next level. Community college programs are competitive, compete for championships, and their coaches promote their athletes to the next level (which doesn't happen for all sports at the high school level).

Earning a certificate from a community college can offer a way to pay for advanced degrees. Many students need to work while in college to fund their education or personal living expenses. Most work minimum wage jobs or even work two or more jobs. If a student took 12-18 months to develop a skill through a community college certification program, they could conceivably work in a new career that would better help them pay for their college education. If they completed an AA-based certificate program (one that provides for both the development of skill and completes all general education requirements for a university) they could also reduce the number of semesters they would need to pay for that education.

There are so many benefits to be considered at the local community colleges. Not only do they make higher education vastly more affordable, but they also offer a plethora of potential career development options. No matter the pathway a teenager wishes to take after high school, the offerings of a community college should be considered.

COMMUNITY COLLEGE CASE STUDIES

STUDENT EXPERIENCE

STUDENT NAME: CODY PHALEN

School Choice: Los Medanos Community College

Program Choice: EMT

Potential Career Pathway: EMT then Paramedic

Decision Maker: I chose this program because it's my passion and what I want to do later in life.

Benefits: This option is free for me, gives me the skills I need, and I get to play sports.

Drawbacks: Nothing so far.

What would you tell upcoming students about how to decide what to do after high school? Make your decision on what you want to do early so you can plan ahead.

Anything Else? Not at this time.

COMMUNITY COLLEGE CASE STUDIES

STUDENT EXPERIENCE

STUDENT NAME: JENNIFER JONES*

School Choice: Florida Community College

Program Choice: Cosmetology and Aesthetics

Potential Career Pathway: Aesthetics

Decision Maker: I had wanted to be a hairstylist since I was a little kid. As an adult, I moved into being an esthetician.

Benefits: The ability to make a good living and the relationships I've cultivated through the years.

Drawbacks: I chose a profession that generally pays via commission. So, when it's good it can be really good. And when it's slow, it impacts your income.

*not their real names

What would you tell upcoming students about how to decide what to do after high school? I would first find out what kinds of things come naturally to you. If you aren't academic and don't care for the social aspect of school either, then finding out what interests you and what you are good at can help direct you to a trade at a community college.

Anything Else? I always knew college wouldn't be for me. The good thing about trades is that you learn a skill you will always use (I still cut hair on the side), and you can do multiple trade skills without breaking the bank. If the first trade doesn't work out, you can go back. And if you're ever in a pinch for a job, you'll have it to fall back on.

COMMUNITY COLLEGE CASE STUDIES

PARENT EXPERIENCE

*Note: parents listed may not be related
to students mentioned above*

PARENT NAME: ALLISON MAYFIELD

School Choice: Cape Fear Community College

Program Choice:
Associate Degree in Automotive Maintenance

Potential Career Pathway:
Automotive maintenance

How did you help your teen with their decision?
I told him to pursue what he loves which is cars.

Benefits: Hands-on learning

Drawbacks: None

**What would you tell parents about how to
help their student decide what to do after high
school?** Let them pursue their own path.

Anything Else? Be sure to fill out the FAFSA even for community colleges. My child qualified for a Pell Grant which is paying for it fully.

COMMUNITY COLLEGE CASE STUDIES

PARENT EXPERIENCE

PARENT NAME: PHYLLIS GATES

School Choice: Trident Technical College

Program Choice: Electrical/Culinary Arts (he did not complete though)

Potential Career Pathway: Possibly child development and youth services

How did you help your teen with their decision? He chose based on his interest and passion for working with children.

Benefits: Easy to change career paths at Trident, minimal financial commitment

Drawbacks: Does not like online classes. No college atmosphere (student activities, etc.).

What would you tell parents about how to help their student decide what to do after high school? Let the child make the decision, not the parents! Help them find their passion (or a job they genuinely enjoy) before they choose a secondary education path.

Anything Else? Sometimes post-high school plans do not include school and that's ok. They just need to understand the importance of a strong work ethic and doing what you enjoy.

COMMUNITY COLLEGE CASE STUDIES

PARENT EXPERIENCE

PARENT NAME: STACY PHALEN

School Choice: Los Medanos Community College

Program Choice: Paramedic/Fire

Potential Career Pathway: To graduate with a 4-year degree in fire safety and become a Fireman.

How did you help your teen with their decision? He started talking about being an EMT in 2019. I had him work with Stephanie the same year and his passion for becoming an EMT grew into pursuing a career as a paramedic as well as possibly a firefighter. He has now developed a plan that fits his need to play sports and gain experience and skill at the same time.

Benefits: He is confident in his decision because it has been his to make all along; we just gave him tools to figure out what he wanted to do.

Drawbacks: Nothing. He is still a senior in high school. One benefit is that he will enroll in a pre-EMT class come spring of 2021 at Contra Costa College.

What would you tell parents about how to help their student decide what to do after high school? Keep it simple. If they do not know, it is OK. Let them explore in college or find a trade.

Anything Else? It's stressful of course, but if your child knows you are there to help them through the process it can make it easier on both of you.

LEARN A SKILL AND (POSSIBLY) GET PAID TO DO IT: APPRENTICESHIP AND TRADE SCHOOL PROGRAMS

Julie* is a client of mine who is interested in the hospitality industry. There are many options available to her, from 4-year Hospitality degrees (she has the requirements to be accepted) to 2-year programs at a local community college. However, Julie, while extremely intelligent, finds traditional schooling tedious. We discussed all her collegiate options, but she was still struggling to find a sense of excitement in any of them. In one session we investigated an apprenticeship program in her area. She found that it not only covered the education requirements and costs of one full year of college, but it also provided a mentor in the industry and would pay her to do the work while she learned. At the end of the two-year program, she would have the opportunity to be hired by her mentor company or search and apply *to other companies with 24 months of experience on her resume…at only 19 years of age. Not only that, but the companies she could work for were willing to pay her to continue earning higher and higher degrees.*

After researching more on her own, Julie determined that this option suited her best. One of her goals is not to go into debt to get an education. Another goal is making the best use of her time. To her, paying thousands of dollars and spending four years in a classroom seemed like a waste of time when she could get paid to learn, gain marketable experience, and be trained in real-time in two.

The truth is that utilizing the benefits of an apprenticeship or trade school program may prove a better investment of time and money for some students than attending a 4-year college right after high school.

Apprenticeship programs are generally two-year programs starting as early as 16 years of age. There are two types of apprenticeship programs: youth (16-18) and adult (19-24). These programs provide college education (dual enrollment courses for high school students) and help participants develop the necessary skills to be successful in a particular industry area. This is in addition to being paid a scalable wage and earning bonuses and raises while they are in the program. What this means is that while teenagers are completing their high school education, covered by the program, they are not only learning industry related skills in real-time but also earning financial stability.

Trade schools are somewhat like community college certification programs in that they offer certification in a specific set of skills. These programs however are generally taught by educators with many years' experience in the field who understand the current needs of the industry. Additionally, these programs often have specific job placement services as well as strong connections with industries to provide internships and jobs for their students. Trade schools are only as good as their graduates, so they are heavily invested in making sure those graduates have the highest level of skill possible to enter the industry they are interested in and meet the ever-changing needs of industry leaders.

Why aren't these types of programs much more interesting to today's high school students? I offer that it's because of a negative stereotype. Unfortunately, many teenagers (and their parents) have come to believe these programs are not as prestigious as attending a fouryear program. While in the past there was an industry-driven demand for qualified candidates to have an advanced degree, today's industry environment is indicating something much different. Industry experts are not looking for those "well-rounded individuals" who can handle a four-year course load. What they are looking for are trained, experienced employees who are willing to learn the ways of their company. While four-year institutions are fantastic at giving background and orienting students to the industry overall, trade schools and apprenticeship programs give teenagers real-time experience in an industry as it continues to evolve.

Here's the Main Idea

The truth is that utilizing the benefits of an apprenticeship or trade school program may prove a better investment of time and money for some students than attending a 4-year college right after high school.

With the rise of tuition year after year, the expense of paying for residence life, and the unknowns of balancing collegiate requirements with social life, many students struggle to make a four-year collegiate experience beneficial for themselves at 17 or 18 years of age. Additionally, those students who are interested in working in an industry that requires a specific skill set may do better starting at a trade school or apprenticeship program than those who attend a four-year institution right after high school.

Why should parents and teens stop and consider these options? According to HVAC Technical Institute:[5]

In a world where hundreds of people apply for the same position, it is important to find a way to stand out. It is one thing to say you are competent in a specific skill, and it is another to prove your qualifications through a specific certification.

Employers understand the significance of these [trade school] certifications and realize the capa-

bilities and skill set that they imply. The more certifications you can put on your resume, the more
appealing you become as a job candidate.

High school students interested in the field of Science,
Technology, Engineering, and Math (STEM), one of the
fastest growing industries to date, may find greater success
in trade and apprenticeship programs as well as greater
abilities to develop advanced degrees. According to the
STEM Jobs website:[6]

> The programs offered at trade schools are often
> shorter and tailored to teach students practical
> skills with the goal of direct employment. Many
> employers will even pay for students to continue
> their trade school education once they join the
> company. A student who enrolls in a trade school
> will typically finish their education more quickly,
> allowing them to join the workforce and begin build-
> ing a career earlier.

This same article also discusses the benefits a student
can gain financially by attending a trade school or apprenticeship program:

> According to the Association for Career and Tech-
> nical Education, graduates with technical or applied
> science associate degrees out-earn bachelor's
> degree holders by an average of $2,000 to
> $11,000. When you think about these earnings of
> a student over 10 years, that amounts to $20,000.

$110,000 more than their classmates who attended four-year universities. When you factor in the amount those students paid for their education, the advanced financial success of those who a tend trade schools and apprenticeship programs is even more pronounced.

In an interview I had with Melissa Stowasser, Assistant Vice President of Community Partnerships for Trident Technical College[7], she shared that the Charleston Regional Youth Apprenticeship Program she works with, while still in relative infancy, is often cited as a national program for other states looking to develop their own apprenticeship programs. It was begun about 7 years ago at the request of a manufacturing company located in Ladson, SC called IFA[8]. In Haldensleben, Germany, where IFA is headquartered, apprenticeship programs are much more valuable than a college degree. When they arrived here and learned there were no apprenticeship programs, they approached Trident Technical College and their partners and began working with them to develop one. The program now includes over 180 companies that represent 18 career pathways and 9 industry sectors.

Of the level of success participants can gain, she cites not only skill development as well as access to utilizing state-of-the-art technology, but also the tremendous earning potential of those in the program. Of the 351 participants hired to date (in only the last 7 years) there have been five individuals between the ages of 19 and 21 who not only earned the skill they needed to work in the industry area they were interested in and were hired by their mentor companies or competitors right after the program ended, they also earned enough money to be able to buy their own homes. Think about that for a minute. Your teenager could conceivably build the experience needed to enter into the industry they are interested in by the time they graduate high school and earn enough money by the time they are 21 to be able to purchase their own home.

In a conversation I had with Chad Vail, the Work-based Learning Partnerships Coordinator for the Charleston County School District[9], he noted that several companies like Bosch and the Charleston Electrical Contractors Association, for example, have had longstanding traditions of apprenticeship programs, and that several opportunities exist for pre-apprenticeships that benefit both students and employers alike:

> [pre-apprenticeships are] custom-designed to prepare individuals to enter and succeed in apprenticeship programs. These programs have many benefits for both employers and participants. For participants, they provide the knowledge and skills training needed for specific jobs and industries and are especially helpful to individuals who may have barriers to employment, such as under represented populations. Employers also benefit by getting screened, trained employees who are ready to work, saving them recruiting time and resources, and reducing turnover rates.

Within my own family, our daughter, who graduated from a four-year university, is finding great happiness in pursuing a trade school. Frustrated with the lack of relevant education and career direction she received from her university, she has determined a trade school will give her the career-specific skills, experience, and customized program she needs to be successful in her own life. She realizes there is increased value for her by earning a four-year degree, but she also understands that had she not spent so much money and time pursuing a degree she's not going to use, she would have been able to pursue this new direction much sooner, earning with it a better wage than she was able to earn while in college working part-time jobs.

Other adults who responded to a question I posted on an online Facebook mom's group page about whether or not they believed college was a valuable experience, overwhelmingly indicated that if that option would make their teenager happy, they would support them. But the majority also indicated their own collegiate experience ended much the same way as my daughter's; unused and forgotten, causing them to be in debt for 10 years or more, and having to pay to develop a specific skill set a completely different way that became much more valuable.

More and more it is becoming evident that considering additional options such as trade schools or apprenticeship programs may benefit students in greater ways than any other option available to them. Therefore, it is worth it for parents and teens to stop for a moment and consider the benefits these options offer in getting them the experience and skill set they need for the potential careers they are interested in.

Who might best be successful in these types of programs? Consider the following scenarios:

✿ **Some students do better in non-traditional education settings.** Some teens thrive in the traditional model, but there is a growing number who do not. Technical schools and apprenticeship programs offer a wide variety of specialty skill development programs that give the opportunity to earn well-paying jobs while spending less time in a classroom setting than traditional education models.

✿ **Some students prefer to work in respectable blue-collar careers.** Most 4-year colleges offer a great liberal arts education, which is good for some careers, but not all. The blue-collar workforce, specialty technical areas, and even IT do not always require a liberal arts education. Without these tradesmen and women much of our functioning society would come to a standstill. Many teens would prefer and, as a result, have a more successful future to use their hands and build skills actively rather than passively.

Some students need to earn a livable wage while in school. Earning a certificate can mean a better job while completing a college education (if needed). Many students need to work while in college to fund their education or personal living expenses. Most work minimum wage jobs or even work two or more jobs. If a high schooler or recent high school graduate took 18 months or so to develop a skill, (a youth apprenticeship program could actually be completed before high school graduation), they could conceivably work in a new career that would better help them pay for their college education. If they completed some college courses while involved in these programs (most apprenticeship programs offer some type of education component: high school courses for those still enrolled in high school, and collegiate courses for those who have graduated), they could also reduce the number of semesters they would need to pay for that education.

 Some students want to start their careers sooner rather than later. Many students have clear ideas about what they want to do with their future but are frustrated by having to spend so much time learning in classrooms that have nothing to do with their future careers. Completing general education courses and industry theory courses may be a waste of time in the face of trade schools and apprenticeship programs for those teenagers who want to start their careers closer to high school graduation than a 4-year degree can offer.

✺ **Some students would prefer to be paid to learn on the job.** Students who apply and are accepted into an apprenticeship program are not only educated (high school students are enrolled in dual enrollment courses), but they're also paid a scalable wage for the two years they are enrolled in the program. While they are working with a mentor in the industry, learning in real-time the skills, character, and networking it takes to be successful in that industry area, they are also earning money. Upon completion of the program, many young adults can become self-sufficient. Think about that, an 18-year-old can be completely self-sufficient and not in debt at all with 2 years of industry experience on their resume.

✺ **Some students may want direct skill development and industry networking.** Trade schools and apprenticeship programs have been around for longer than formal liberal arts college education programs. Traditionally a way for people to learn a trade in real-time, these programs offer opportunities for skill development, industry networking, and education that goes far beyond the classroom. These programs offer young adults the opportunity to support themselves, develop marketable skills, and enter the work-force much sooner than 4-year programs, all while being able to learn first-hand from industry mentors and personnel, rather than in theory, how an industry works.

There are so many benefits to be considered at the local trade schools and apprenticeship programs, especially for students who do not have a specific passion for a future career that requires a 4-year degree or who do not like school to begin with. This option may provide career pathway clarification, development of financial stability (which can help fund any future education needs), career networking opportunities, and even time to develop personally.

STUDENT EXPERIENCE

STUDENT NAME: TIMOTHY BEER

School Choice:
Southeast Lineman Training Center

Program Choice: Electrical Line Worker Program

Potential Career Pathway: Journeyman Lineman

Decision Maker: I was interested in heights and climbing.

Benefits: Experience and knowledge

Drawbacks: Out of work to attend school

What would you tell upcoming students about how to decide what to do after high school?
Look into the trades and the benefits that come with them. Don't let high school teachers tell you college is the only way you'll be successful.

Anything Else? My school was only for 15 weeks and I have never learned so much in such a short period of time and have never been put in a greater position to be successful in life and the trade.

STUDENT EXPERIENCE

STUDENT NAME: CORINNA CHRISTOPHER

School Choice: Trident Technical College Youth Apprenticeship Program

Program Choice:
Bookkeeping/Accounting Certificate

Potential Career Pathway: Mathematics

Decision Maker: I have always been interested in Math and Business so when I heard about this program that would build my resume, give me college credit, and real-world experience, I was eager to pursue it.

Benefits: The most beneficial part of my decision was getting a job I love and is helping me make decisions about my future career path.

Drawbacks: The only drawback is the fact that I had to stop playing sports my senior year to make time for my classes.

What would you tell upcoming students about how to decide what to do after high school? Find a paid apprenticeship in a field you're interested in! It's the best way to gain experience and confidence in deciding the best path for you.

Anything Else? I found through this apprenticeship that although I love business, accounting specifically is not my calling. I love math and am passionate about it so I will be pursuing a degree in mathematics. However, I am extremely grateful for this internship because it helped me make decisions and gave me a loving work environment.

APPRENTICESHIP AND TRADE SCHOOLS CASE STUDIES

STUDENT EXPERIENCE

STUDENT NAME: ROBERT PAIGE

School Choice: Trident Technical College Youth Apprenticeship Program

Program Choice: Industrial Mechanics

Potential Career Pathway: Currently working as a Machinery Technician in the United States Coast Guard

Decision Maker: I wanted a head start in my career and the youth program gave me a great opportunity to do so.

Benefits: I was able to use the skills/knowledge I obtained in the program to accelerate my career and get the job I wanted.

Drawbacks: There were no drawbacks for me.

What would you tell upcoming students about how to decide what to do after high school? Don't let other people make you think college is the only way to a successful career. There are many great opportunities out there in the trade environment that will allow you to learn a valuable set of skills that will lead to success.

Anything Else? The military has great career opportunities.

APPRENTICESHIP AND TRADE SCHOOLS CASE STUDIES

STUDENT EXPERIENCE

STUDENT NAME: DRAKE HEAD

School Choice: Trident Technical College Youth Apprenticeship Program

Program Choice: Mechanical Engineering

Potential Career Pathway: Mechanical Engineer

Decision Maker: Engineering Teacher in high school/friends of mine in the youth apprenticeship

Benefits: Working in an industry surrounded by Engineers

Drawbacks: Calculus classes

What would you tell upcoming students about how to decide what to do after high school? An internship is not only the best way to get your foot in the door at large corporations but also gain invaluable knowledge about the field you want to be in.

Anything Else? Make sure to follow your ambitions and strive to excel in everything you do.

PARENT EXPERIENCE

*Note: parents listed may not be related
to students mentioned above*

PARENT NAME: MARY BEAL

School Choice: Charleston Regional Youth Apprenticeships Program

Program Choice: Mechanical Engineering - B.A.

Potential Career Pathway: Mechanical Engineer

How did you help your teen with their decision?
(edited for space) Our son has always been interested in putting things together and taking them apart both ways usually as intended, but not always. He had the opportunity to do a summer internship at Bosch in Stuttgart, Germany, which he enjoyed. His next great opportunity was winning a spot with the Charleston Regional Apprenticeship Program for a two-year position at Bosch here in Charleston, SC. During those two years, he worked 10 hours per week at Bosch, took his normal high school

classes and classes at Trident Technical College. Our son applied to 5 universities and was accepted at all 5. He was awarded over $400,000 in combined scholarship money. He chose a school and was able to transfer 12 hours from Trident Tech to his new school. At this point, one might be thinking our son is a stellar student, top of his class. A great guy, but no, not a stellar student. He was diagnosed with dysgraphia, attended a school that specialized in educating students with learning differences, then entered mainstream public school in 8th grade. There is no doubt that his hands-on, practical TTC Apprenticeship Program made it possible for him to be a successful college student.

Benefits: The apprenticeship allowed him to see what going straight into the workforce after high school graduation might be like. We feel he made a much more informed decision based on his wishes, not ours.

Drawbacks: There have been no drawbacks. It was win/win in every way.

What would you tell parents about how to help their students decide what to do after high school? We would recommend that parents encourage their children to experience as many diverse school, work, volunteer, and play options as possible. Many options are free or paid. The experience they gain will help them make better decisions about what they would like to do with their lives.

Anything Else? It is sometimes difficult to encourage your child to try different things when you know that they may not make the choices you would have made for them. However, we hope providing the scope and encouragement to explore ideas will lead to happier adults.

APPRENTICESHIP AND TRADE SCHOOLS CASE STUDIES

PARENT EXPERIENCE

PARENT NAME: SHARON LEE

School Choice: Trident Technical College Youth Apprenticeship Program

Program Choice: CNA/ PCT/ RN

Potential Career Pathway: Nursing

How did you help your teen with their decision? I didn't; it was something she chose on her own. I just encouraged her and helped lead her in the direction that would land her on this path.

Benefits: Financial freedom/Working at MUSC as an Apprentice PCT

Drawbacks: Well given 2020, it's been having to move to strictly online sessions. Also, the newness of the Apprenticeship program involving MUSC has been challenging because not everyone has been on the same page regarding policy and procedures and it's been somewhat frustrating.

What would you tell parents about how to help their students decide what to do after high school? Talk to your child about their desires for a career. Give them resources or have them research what that career is really about and see if they truly are interested. Once they've decided which career they'd like to choose, be supportive and help them get to where they want to go with their career choice. I would also let them know that failure may occur and failing is a part of life; what's important though is not quitting. Getting back up and continuing on the path you've chosen until you succeed. Be your child's biggest cheerleader. Let them know YOU believe in them, and that will help them believe in themselves.

Anything Else? Know your child and how they tick. Encourage their abilities and strengths rather than focusing on their weakness. They need to know that you are behind them 100% in their endeavors to be successful in their choice of a career field.

APPRENTICESHIP AND TRADE SCHOOLS CASE STUDIES

PARENT EXPERIENCE

PARENT NAME: AMY KOSAR

School Choice: Trident Technical College Youth Apprenticeship Program

Program Choice: Associate of Applied Science, Hospitality & Tourism Management

Potential Career Pathway: Event Planning

How did you help your teen with their decision?
As a rising Junior in high school, Carson was not sure what path she wanted. She learned about the Youth Apprenticeship Program at Trident Technical College and decided to enter the program with a vague interest in hospitality.

Benefits: She learned so much about the hospitality industry and found that she was extremely interested in event planning.

Drawbacks: No drawbacks at all.

What would you tell parents about how to help their students decide what to do after high school? I would and do tell parents; look at the TTC YAP. Free College and books. They can gain job experience. There is nothing to lose!!

Anything Else? I am so glad that she found the YAP. It has helped her to find an otherwise un-decided path.

PARENT EXPERIENCE

PARENT NAME: BLAKE CROSBY

School Choice: Charleston Regional Youth Apprenticeship Program

Program Choice: Computer Networking

Potential Career Pathway:
Career in information technology

How did you help your teen with their decision?
Based on his interests and potential for jobs

Benefits: Gaining confidence to navigate in a workplace environment. Learning to deal with driving to work, managing money, and taking responsibility for communicating with his supervisor.

Drawbacks: Missed opportunities for other after school activities.

What would you tell parents about how to help their students decide what to do after high school? Make sure they are pursuing a pathway they are interested in and not just to appease the parent or check a box for a school application

Anything Else? I think it is important to keep good communication with your child about how their experience is going. In my experience, the technical aspect of the job was the easiest, but he did need guidance in navigating the more "soft skill" aspects of the job.

JOINING THE MILITARY AFTER HIGH SCHOOL HAS MORE BENEFITS THAN YOU THINK

Richard Maldonado-Rodrigues* was an average student in high school who originally set out to work his way through his local community college before transferring to a 4-year college. Halfway through his first year his funding ran out and he was left with a decision: go into debt to fund his education, drop out, or join the military. He chose the Navy and committed to 8 years. Upon the end of his contract, he will use the GI bill, which will cover three full years of tuition and provide a housing stipend, to finish his degree in psychology.

In my conversation with him, I learned that not only did the Navy help him with his education, but they also paid him a salary, provided housing and food stipends, and

---

*The names in this chapter are real

he now qualifies for lifetime benefits. He did deploy for 2 years, but since his field was mental health care, he served Naval personnel, not on the front lines.

Zachary Moseley, currently a retired Veteran, chose to follow in the footsteps of his grandfather and father. He enlisted in the Navy at first to enter the nuclear program, but before starting changed to mental health.

In my conversation with him I learned he committed to an 8-year enlistment and in that time had been trained as an EMT and gained years of experience as the EMT support for the Women's 4th Battalion at Parris Island. Upon retirement, Zach chose to use his GI benefits to pursue a degree in health sciences and has recently been hired by the Navy as a civilian contractor to work at their naval base in Goose Creek, SC.

When students consider their plans after high school, very few explore the military as a viable option, possibly missing out on one of the greatest life decisions they could ever make.

Most teens, when asked the inevitable "What do you want to do after high school?" rarely seem to reply with "Join the military." I wish I knew why this was as the more I explore the opportunities available to today's youth the more it makes sense to consider this option as equal to a 4-year college or community college/trade school program.

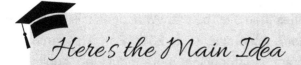

Here's the Main Idea

When students consider their plans after high school, very few explore the military as a viable option, possibly missing out on one of the greatest life decisions they could ever make.

I have met many adults and teenagers who have considered all the options available to them and determined the military was their best fit. Many chose this option to learn specialized skills that would help them in their future careers. Others chose this option to fund their education while also becoming specialized. Several joined because they did not want to continue their formal "book learning" and preferred a more hands-on approach to developing skills for a trade. Still others joined out of a sense of adventure, a sense of tradition, and a sense of duty to their country, especially after the tragedy of 9/11. No matter what reason they gave for joining, they all indicated that joining the military was a massive sacrifice for them and their families. However, they all also shared that they gained so much more than they ever could have in any other option.

The military is stepping up its game to become a serious contender for today's high school graduate with the addition of its new Space Force as well as the enhancement of Special Operations groups. The military is now more tech-savvy, cutting-edge, and engaged in developing new career opportunities than ever before. What does this mean for your teenager? According to a 2017 Pew Research study[10], the military is producing more educated adults than those not in the military: "More than eight-in-ten DOD active-duty officers have at least a bachelor's degree... They are four times as likely as average adults ages 18 to 44 to have completed a postgraduate degree [and]... The vast majority of enlisted personnel (92%) have completed high school or some college. **This compares with 60% of all U.S. adults ages 18 to 44.**" (*emphasis mine*).

In an interview I conducted on Oct. 20, 2020, with Captain Robin Lewis of the US Navy[11], her experience in the Navy suggests that this number is higher. According to her "I don't know any officer, not a one, that does not have a college degree..."

In short, research and experience show that the military produces higher educated adults than those not in the military.

Most parents assume joining the military automatically means their teenager is heading to the front lines of any wars our nation may be involved in. While this is certainly a major consideration, there are other ways of serving in the military than on the front lines. While each branch has different options, all need medical staff, cybersecurity technicians, mechanics, chefs, police, paperwork processors, etc., in addition to active-duty service members who may serve their communities, states, or regions in various support capacities.

According to Captain Lewis, "Basically, almost any discipline that you find outside of the military, you find in the military. Think of an aircraft carrier, for example, as a city. There is a store (shop keep rating), galley (culinary specialist rating), barbershop (which is a sub-specialty under shopkeeping), supplies (purchasing agents), a chapel (chaplains and chaplain assistance), and the list goes on: fire department, training/teaching, police (including dog handlers), veterinarians, air traffic controllers, weather people..."

This perspective can help today's teenagers, and their parents, think beyond "deployment" and see the many opportunities available to them.

Additionally, with the creation of the GI Bill,[12] any service member who serves four or more years is eligible to have up to 100% of three years of their higher education paid for (most recruits can complete at least one year of college credit while enlisted in their first term, for free), with various other tuition assistance options available to them. Finally, service members are paid, with benefits, for their time. According to an article by The Military Wallet,[13] a newly enlisted service member earns ~$20,000 per year while a new second lieutenant starts with ~$36,000 per year, both with full benefits. This is in addition to living expenses being covered by the military as well. And, if a service member so desires, (and their post allows) they can serve, get paid, and attend school at the same time on the military's dime. (As with any organization, military pay, and benefits, is a complex process. For more specific details according to rank and class, please visit https://militarypay.defense.

gov/pay/.) In a time when teens (and parents) are wondering if the cost of other higher education programs is worth it, this option presents itself as a financial boon and should be seriously considered.

However, there are some downsides as well. The military is after the best, (as are 4-year colleges) so they have eligibility requirements that need to be met before anyone can join. According to an article about joining the military on USA.gov,[14] there are health and fitness, citizenship, age, testing, and education minimum requirements that need to be met. Upon researching more I learned that several common medical issues will make a student at worst ineligible to join, and at best have to postpone joining for 6 months or more. However, this does not have to be a life-long deterrent. If a teen does have a medical condition they may think is limiting, they should consult with a recruiter as there are waivers for health conditions.

The military is referred to as a service industry because it is. Those who join do so in service to their country and its citizens. This means they must sacrifice for the good of others. Not all teenagers are ready for this level of dedication. While contracts can be as short as four years, that may be a long time for an 18-year-old to give up their personal desires. According to Master Sergeant Jorge Cortijo of the United States Air Force, (who joined as a 17-year-old high school student as a result of the tragedy of 9/11) "you give way more than you get but what you get is incredibly valuable."

The biggest downside, of course, is the potential risk of loss of life. Serving our country on the front lines in any capacity has its risks. Fighting in wars in countries all over the world, standing up for freedom and democracy in areas of unrest, and even attending to the sick and injured after a natural catastrophe all put a teenager in harm's way. However, this is also the only option for which a student's death is accounted for. According to this article from the Military Wallet:[15]

> In the unlikely event of a service member's death, the military or the VA provides a lifetime of benefits for your survivors. The surviving family is given an immediate $100,000 death gratuity benefit, a $400,000 lump sum life insurance benefit (if the member opts into the life insurance), social security and indemnity monthly payments for years, and the transferability of many VA benefits.

There is a lot to consider with this option for a high school student to determine whether it is viable for them. **Here are a few things parents can encourage their teen to consider before making any decision for, or against, this option:**

⚜ **Have your teen research all branches of the military.** Each branch offers different experiences, support for future education, and careers. Each also has a different focus for their service to the country and the world. One recruit told me that the Army and the Marines largely serve as our nation's fighting force, while the Navy and Air Force largely play a supporting role. A student would do well becoming familiar with each before deciding. Have them check out us.gov/join-military for a comprehensive breakdown.

Ⅲ ✪ Encourage your teen to interview at least one veteran or active-duty service member (or more). Who else can give them the true inside experience than someone who's "been there"? Veterans and active-duty service members come in all types, with all kinds of experiences. Try to help them find and interview one in each branch, or at least one in each branch they are interested in.

Ⅲ ✪ Have your teen explore the requirements for eligibility. It's one thing to research and decide on a branch, and it's another thing to be eligible. Encourage your teen to become familiar with requirements like having a high school diploma or GED, physical fitness requirements, medical disqualifiers, and testing. The us.gov/join-military website is a great place to start.

Ⅲ ✪ Have your teen learn the differences between their options. There are multiple ways to join our nation's military forces: enlisting,[16] enrolling in an ROTC program,[17] or attending a service academy.[18] For those who decide a different option is the best fit for them right after high school, they can still consider joining a military branch later in life to help pay for higher education and advanced degrees. Working professionals can enroll in the military post-graduation, usually as an officer.

Have your teen prepare a list of questions to use when meeting with recruiters. Just like preparing for a job interview, it is essential that your teen does their homework and comes prepared (see the Next Steps Guide in the next section of this book for more on this). Determining potential career paths, researching the opportunities of each branch they are interested in, and preparing a list of questions helps make sure your teen fully understands what they may be signing up for.

Have your teen set up an appointment to talk with a recruiter. This will need to be done for each branch they are interested in. If possible, attend with them or <u>at least</u> make sure another adult with their best interests in mind goes with them. Recruiters are essentially salespeople whose goal is to enroll as many recruits as possible. This does not mean they will strong arm your teenager, but they will press them to commit. Prepare your teen to go in with an open mind and always remember you are free to walk out without signing anything and come back later.

Have your teen process all their options before signing. Once a military contract of commitment is signed, it is legally binding. Unlike 4- or 2-year colleges, sports programs, and trade schools, your teen can't choose to change their mind once they have committed. Before making any decision, be sure to have your teen process all their options to determine whether this is right for them.

Joining the military, either right after high school, as part of a collegiate ROTC program, or even through admission to a service academy, is a decision that takes time to make, maybe even more than any other option. There are a multitude of benefits for both our teens and the culture in which we live. Before committing to any other option teens would do well to consider the career, leadership, and financial benefits this option could provide.

STUDENT EXPERIENCE

STUDENT NAME: KIERIGAN MCEVOY

Program Choice:
Army ROTC at the University of Western Kentucky

Are you using the military to help pay for further education? Yes

Degree You are Pursuing: Mandarin Chinese and International Affairs with a minor in Military Science

Decision Maker: I watched two of my neighbors (both girls) go through the ROTC program and saw all the opportunities it opened to them. I wanted to do something active in college that would aid in helping to pay for school, but also help me have a job after graduating. The ROTC seemed like the perfect fit to feed my craving for athletics while also doing something logical to help my future career. I think it is also very humbling to be a part of something bigger than yourself.

Did you meet with a recruiter? Yes

What was that experience like? I met with several recruiters. One from the National Guard and several from various schools I was looking at to pursue an education. Overall, each visit was highly informative and gave me all my options spelled out extensively. The thing is, if you don't speak military, some of these options and information being said to you seem like it's a good deal. The recruiters are all genuinely nice and helpful but at the end of the day, they are salesmen. So, I was thankful I had people I know in the military to fact check with. I liked each recruiter I met with and never felt too pressured into any decision.

What was your end goal for joining the military after high school? I wanted to find a way to pay for myself, to take care of my schooling. I started looking at the ROTC program and thought to myself, "this is a good deal I don't know why more people don't do this." Now that I'm enrolled in the program, I would say so far it is worth it and highly recommend it to anyone. I also think having a military background only helps with a professional career. People hiring you know that you were held to a different standard in college and the military, so they are more likely to trust you as a worker.

Benefits: By joining Army ROTC I've been able to have something to work towards, a reason to go to the gym, a reason to get my homework done early, and go to sleep because physical training starts at 0545 in the morning. The most beneficial aspect of my decision so far is that I feel like I belong somewhere, I have a team. I have something to work towards. Being 5 hours away from home and not knowing anyone sucks, but because of ROTC, I have something to keep me going.

Drawbacks: Choosing ROTC over playing college soccer has been the hardest decision of my life.

What would you tell upcoming students about how to decide what to do after high school? College is not for everyone. College in the traditional sense is not for everyone. College athletics is not for everyone. And just because you choose not to go to traditional college does not make you a failure either. There are so many opportunities out there for students after high school. I don't want anyone to think that college is the only option like schools have led us to believe. It's not, and you're not a failure for choosing something else for yourself.

Anything Else? For a long time, I struggled with watching my friends commit to college teams. I thought people would look at them in their success and then look at me and assume I wasn't as good as them because I wasn't committed. I spent so much time putting myself down and struggling with a decision I knew was best for me, but instead, I was worried about if it was best for everyone else. Never do that. Never take what you know is right for you and compare it to what others expect from you. As much as I miss soccer, I wouldn't change my decision.

STUDENT EXPERIENCE

STUDENT NAME: MAXWELL HIRSHMAN

Program Choice: Army Active Duty (Enlist)

Are you using the military to help pay for further education? Yes

Degree you are pursuing: Business

Decision Maker: After realizing I had no passion or motivation and was working a lame job, I decided to get out of my parents' house. I needed some fresh air and a fresh state of mind.

Did you meet with a recruiter? Yes

What was the experience like? Recruiters push for quotas. However, if you do your research about the field/job you want to join it'll benefit you a lot in advance and will save a lot of BS talk with the recruiter (who just needs you as a number) They do their job well with what they're given though and provide information on whatever you ask, you just have to know what to ask.

What was your end goal of joining the military after high school? GI Bill (college tuition) and self-discipline

Benefits: It's helped me afford a newer car and has given me a new outlook on life. Not having to worry about student loans is a bonus too.

Drawbacks: It's a commitment because it takes away from your youth if you join at an early age. All the people I graduated with have degrees or are in their 3rd/4th year of college.

What would you tell upcoming students about how to decide what to do after high school? Sometimes not all of us are ready to do the generic 4-year leap into college. Some people operate differently. Don't be ashamed to take a gap year and figure out what you need to do, and/or work and save money.

Anything Else? Know what job you want to do. Do something that benefits not only your passion but your career after service. Many vets get out that joined as a combatant (i.e., infantry, scout, tanker) and find it hard to even qualify for a civilian job because their MOS (military occupation specialty) didn't teach them much but to shoot and kill (I'm a 19K, tanker, for reference). If you do join, use your off time to take college classes or any military classes to improve yourself as an individual.

MILITARY CASE STUDIES

PARENT EXPERIENCE

Note: parents listed may not be related
to students mentioned above

PARENT NAME: AMY MCEVOY

Program Choice: Army ROTC

How did your teen make their decision?
She was offered full tuition, had several schools to choose from, and saw many advantages and opportunities in college and after graduation: life experiences, structure, team, leadership, contacts, travel, service

How did you help your teen with their decision?
My daughter wanted to be part of a soccer team and she thought she might want to study Chinese. That's all I had to go by, so I started researching. Chinese was the best place to start. That led me to the Chinese Flagship program. We have friends with children who did ROTC, so I researched that as well. I found that ROTC and the Flagship program when used together have some amazing opportunities. Well, none of this had anything to do with

soccer so we had a little problem. My daughter is athletic. A team player. Competitive. Gives 100% daily. Wants to be around others who are like her. But she is not a D1 athlete and most of the flagship schools are D1. While researching and listening to others talk about ROTC, she decided to take a chance and apply for a National ROTC scholarship. She still had not given up on the dream of playing soccer in college though. We applied to over 10 schools. Some with ROTC. Some with Chinese. Some with soccer hopes. We visited 6 of these schools, one over ten hours away. I made a spreadsheet with all the info on each school: deadlines, ACT/GPA, scholarships, majors, ROTC, soccer, and cost. We would go over and over it. We would visit the schools again. It was always going to be her decision, but I knew I needed to be there to help reassure her that whatever her choice was, it would be okay. I believe I needed to be there to help her figure out where she 'didn't' want to go. Through long talks, bouts of arguments, and plus-and-minus charts, I constantly reminded my daughter of what kind of person she was. What she liked in others. What she wanted out of life. ROTC isn't soccer but it is everything soccer stands for and a whole lot more. I hope I helped her see that.

Benefits: She has had the opportunity to be on a team. She thrives in this atmosphere. Also, the leadership that comes from the ROTC staff-teachers is unbelievable. They are there to see them succeed.

Drawbacks: Nothing really- we had to give up playing soccer and being close to home. But the benefits outweigh that.

What would you tell parents about how to help their students decide what to do after high school? Explore all options and opportunities but be realistic. Set boundaries on finance but explore money options. There are tons of scholarships out there for everything. Make charts, spread sheets, and pros and cons lists. Then have lots of discussions (good or bad) with your child. Don't start too early but don't wait till August of their senior year. I would rather my daughter explore all options than regret not doing so later. She feels solid in her decision now and I believe that's why. Be supportive! For some students, this is the hardest decision to make. The worry of making the wrong decision sets very heavy on their minds. I believe in reassuring students that changing their minds is okay. Deciding to come home, attended a different school or vocation is common and nothing to fear.

Anything Else? It's hard. At least it was for my daughter. Some kids are easy (my son will be) so hopefully, you know your child and what your child needs from you. My daughter needed compassion. She also needed to be pushed. She would have excelled anywhere but she needed to decide where she 'fit.' We can't always be certain where our decisions lead us or if we will have to make new ones, but through prayer and knowing some-one in a higher place is really in charge helps me to know everything will turn out as it should.

MILITARY CASE STUDIES

PARENT EXPERIENCE

PARENT NAME: DIANA HIRSHMAN

Program Choice: Army, Active Duty

How did your teen make their decision? He realized he needed a change in his life...for the good. Goals were set up before enlisting a if he didn't follow through with them, then the agreement was to join the military. He came up with a list of 3 things. He'd start with the first and if he failed, he'd move to the 2nd, and so on. 1st Step: Enroll in Trident Tech - get an associate degree in computer science. (He went one semester then dropped out) 2nd Step: Kohls- climb the ladder. He eventually realized management wasn't for him. 3rd Step: Army

How did you help your teen with their decision? There was lots of compromising and grace. To start, his dad and I wanted him to realize the military is what he needed but we needed our son to buy into this "grand" plan. It took about a year but in the end, Max will tell you in a heartbeat, that was the best thing for him.

Benefits: He needed structure in his life and to also be pushed out of his comfort zone. He went from being terrified to order pizza to communicating with Polish and German people who didn't speak a lick of English, navigating through large airports on his own, and surviving in brutal climate conditions while overseas all because he did not have a choice. The Army has whipped his body and mind into shape and is teaching him the value of respect and honor and he now definitely appreciates the simple things in life.

Drawbacks: Not being able to come home for the holidays.

What would you tell parents about how to help their students decide what to do after high school? I would advise that all children are different and to be patient but firm with the goals that are set after high school. I think there's a balance with helping your child decide what comes after high school, but I would suggest parents stand strong and hold them accountable. For each of my children I would make sure they had all the resources they needed to make an educated decision on what to do after high school... from job shadowing, internships, college tours, etc. It's exhausting but necessary.

Anything Else? No

PARENT EXPERIENCE

PARENT NAME: DANA MINOR

Program Choice: Trident Technical College Youth Apprenticeship Program, IT Security Certificate, NAVY - IT SUBMARINES

How did your teen make their decision?
I suggested he consider it, but the rest was all him.

How did you help your teen with their decision?
Honestly, he had no path and hadn't applied to any colleges, so I told him to try this.

Benefits: It gave him a starting point, work experience, and a taste of the real world.

Drawbacks: My child was lazy and did not pursue his Associates in IT.

What would you tell parents about how to help their students decide what to do after high school? Weigh all your options, look at the cost, and what that money will buy. Then decide together.

Sometimes parents might have to be pushy like I was because it's hard to send your super smart but super lazy kid to an apprenticeship program versus college when you are not sure if the 2 years will be a waste of time. I am grateful for this program because it was a great way for my son to get his feet wet in IT.

Anything Else? START EARLY!

MILITARY CASE STUDIES

PARENT EXPERIENCE

PARENT NAME: PAIGE HOWELL (Child #1)

School Choice: University of Florida

Program Choice: Business

Potential Career Pathway: Military

How did you help your teen with their decision?
I listened, helped him sort through choices and outcomes, and supported his decision.

Benefits: No student debt for him or us, with ROTC scholarships, and a guaranteed job.

Drawbacks: He does not have much control over his life for the next 8 - 10 years

What would you tell parents about how to help their students decide what to do after high school? Know there is no one right path. Help your student choose THEIR right path!

CAN A GAP SEASON BE BENEFICIAL? YES!

Jessica,* a client of mine, is a high school senior completely turned off by the idea of college. As she entered her senior year her parents noticed a growing lack of motivation and disinterest in school, her future, and life in general that bothered them. They had discussed the idea of a gap season and, while not unsupportive, they did not know how to trust that a gap season would lead to anything beneficial for their daughter. They worried she would "fall behind" or end up on the couch with nothing to motivate her. In their minds, continuing schooling at least guaranteed she would be doing something productive with her time, even though their daughter seemed disinterested in that option.

In our sessions together Jessica and I explored the options after high school available to her. The traditional choices, in her perspective, felt like long-term prison sen-

tences of boredom. As we explored her passions and dreams, we uncovered several ideas that had been brewing but because she didn't know how to go about developing those ideas into viable options, she had stuffed them down. Once we had those ideas identified, we broke them into skills she would need, and she was able to create a viable plan for a very productive gap season that allowed her to step into any one of her dream careers.

Together with her parents, she is now happily and enthusiastically planning to participate in a gap season program that fits her need for adventure, multi-cultural experiences, relationship building, and her love of marine life, which is creating for her a much more positive attitude to completing her senior year.

Gap seasons (often referred to as gap years, which can be a misnomer), taking a break from formal schooling to learn and gain experience, are increasing in popularity, but can they be beneficial?

According to the Gap Year Association,[19] a gap season is "A semester or year of experiential learning, typically taken after high school and prior to career or post-secondary education, in order to deepen one's practical, professional, and personal awareness."

While this sounds good, practically speaking how does one build a year (or semester) that "deepens their practical, professional and personal awareness" at 17 or 18 years of age?

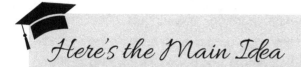

Here's the Main Idea

While it is tough to believe that a typical 17- or 18-year-old can effectively plan to utilize their time well in an unstructured environment, gap seasons can work for some teens. The catch? Parents and their teens need to work together to create a solid plan.

There is a lot of confusion about the benefits or even the purpose of a gap season. Recently made popular by Malia Obama, among others, the discussion has largely centered on whether a teenager can be successful at one.

While it is tough to believe that a typical 17- or 18-year-old can effectively plan to utilize their time well in an unstructured environment, gap seasons can work for some teens. The catch? Parents and their teens need to work together to create a solid plan. Without a structured, well thought out plan, many gap seasons fail to produce the results teens, and their parents, hope for.

There are a multitude of possibilities when planning a gap season that largely depends on a teen's passions, values, and dreams about what their future could be. Many gap seasons are based on developing or sharing their faith and usually center around mission trips or faith-based programs to enrich a teen's relationship with their religion. Others can be part of organized programs that center on experiential learning, providing certifications and even formal classes in a particular area with real hands-on experiences. Still others are based on gaining skill and work experience in a particular industry as part of an apprenticeship program, internship opportunity, or developed through a teen's leg work at securing a position in a company they are interested in. Finally, some can be less formally organized, designed by the teen to create a unique route into their chosen career path.

The truth is a gap season can be as unique as the teen choosing to pursue one, which makes it both exciting and a bit overwhelming. For the teen needing structure, a program may be their best fit. For one who is willing and able to create their own, a more personalized plan may be just what they need.

There are drawbacks of course. Poorly planned seasons can result in a teen not gaining the experience they need, a waste of resources, and a stall in their career development.

So, how do parents and their teens determine whether a gap season can be an effective option? I believe it starts with the actual teenager. **Teens who would do well to take a gap season can fall into one of several categories:**

▌ **Those who have a clearly defined view of their future career for whom the additional experience will add leverage.** These teenagers are highly motivated and know exactly what type of career they want in life. These teens would do well to network with others, serve with others, and seek out specific internships to develop leverage in getting hired at a company in their chosen industry.

In this case, a gap season plan that is based on a specialized internship, apprenticeship, or other career development program can make your teen much more competitive. This type of gap season can be a summer before college, an in-between season between graduation and starting college for up to a whole year (or more), a study abroad program during a college semester or year off, a sabbatical from college after general education requirements are fulfilled, or even taken after college graduation before seeking full-time employment.

 Those for whom a college degree is not necessary and experience in the industry may lead to full-time employment without it. These teens may be interested in the trades or other industry areas for which a degree is not required. While certifications are often necessary, taking time to experience life in a chosen trade area before committing to a certification program would allow these students to better understand their chosen industry, network with future employers, build a solid skills base, and develop a clearer picture of opportunities for career advancement that may influence the decision for future schooling.

In this case, a gap season can be an apprenticeship, internship, or work experience that starts in high school, fills the summer after graduation, spans a semester or whole year before starting a certification program, or comes after a certification. This is also sometimes considered a paid internship in which a company may hire an untrained employee and invest in their development and continued education to bring them on full-time.

Those who need to take a break from formal schooling and/or are driven to serve. These teens may have done exceptionally well in high school, or not, but they may be burned out and need a break or have the heart to step away from their desires in order to serve others. For these students a gap season makes sense for several reasons: it can be a physical way to leave behind their stress and overwhelm; it can be a way to invest in causes and community development opportunities they are passionate about; and it may give them a way to see more of what the world has to offer them in an unstructured way which can enhance their worldview, creativity, and even skill development. Each of these experiences can become a source of inspiration that leads to a career.

In this case, a plan that focuses on a faith-based program (as in a missions trip), with a non-profit organization, as part of the peace corps, or in another service-based capacity can help your teen regroup, reassess their priorities, and establish their plans for their future.

 Those who want to go to college but cannot yet afford it and are motivated to find entry-level employment in their chosen profession. These teens do not want to go into debt to fund their education and do not qualify for as much student aid or scholarship money as they need. They may enroll in a local community college if they can afford it to get some classes completed towards a degree or certification and lessen their overall expenses, but they are chiefly motivated to build experience while building wealth to be able to fund their educational needs.

In this case, a gap season plan that focuses on gaining full-time employment (preferably in the industry of their future career) and keeping their expenses low (like living at home) can help your teenager avoid debt and develop a clearer picture of their career pathway.

 Those who have no idea what to do with the next phase of their lives and are not driven to continue formal education. These teens are burned out by traditional schooling. They may have been labeled poor students because they didn't fit the model of traditional schooling and are struggling with the thought of more of the same. These teens are also those who have not yet developed a definition for themselves of success. They are often overwhelmed by the thought of having to decide on a career for the rest of their lives at 17 and struggle to do so.

In this case, a gap season plan that focuses on helping them identify their gifts, talents, and strengths, learn how to utilize them in various ways, and directs them into developing a successful future can be hugely beneficial. Not only can it help them better understand themselves and increase self-confidence and self-awareness, but it can also help them save time and money by allowing them to explore in a non-binding way before committing to something that may not be a good fit for them.

While a gap season is not suitable for every teen, it is worthy of consideration simply to establish options and allow your teenager to choose for themselves. What is essential for any teen who may be considering this option is a well-structured plan complete with timelines, goals, specific opportunities, and a cost breakdown. Whether that plan is created by a formal organization or independently by the graduate, a well laid out plan can lead to success.

GAP SEASON CASE STUDIES

STUDENT EXPERIENCE

STUDENT NAME: ELLA GRACE BRADLEY

Program Choice: Gap Force Marine Expedition and Dive Instructor Course (https://gapforce.org/us/gap-year-programs/program/marine-expedition-dive-instructor-course)

What do you hope to learn from your gap season? My gap year plan is to travel as far and as wide as possible. I have narrowed it down to a couple of options including a 10-week scuba diving program in Costa Rica that I'm leaning towards. Living in a homestay with roommates while getting your Dive Masters certification and living the Pura Vida lifestyle sounds like an adventure and experience that could help lead me towards other dreams. In this program, I hope to gain more experience and a better understanding of what I want for my future.

Potential Career Pathway: I want to work in hospitality and tourism so I would love to get a feel of what category of job I am looking for in this field.

Decision Maker: Mrs. Haynes has helped me SO much in narrowing my options down. Her mind is open to so many ideas and reveals a whole new path I didn't know was there. I'm a very indecisive person and she has given me the push I need.

Benefits: I can feel the stress melting away with every session because I know I'm that much closer to deciding what my life will look like after high school. It gives me such peace of mind knowing I am going to be able to do what I want.

Drawbacks: It makes me feel as if I make one decision, I may miss out on another. I overthink it and sometimes talk myself out of it because I don't think it will be perfect, but in reality, I'll never know till I get there.

What would you tell upcoming students about how to decide what to do after high school? GO WITH WHAT YOU WANT!! Many people have told me to just wait until senior year and I will want to go to college, but the time never presented itself. I go to a school that identifies you as a college student junior year and works to prepare you for every aspect of college. It is hard to digress from this path, but I did it with pride. I set myself up for success by keeping up good grades even if it didn't matter after high school. I don't want to limit myself and want to be able to keep my options open. Listen to yourself and what your gut is telling you to do.

Anything Else? High school helped me realize my life is so much bigger than teenage drama and school; there is so much more after this, and I can't wait to start it.

STUDENT EXPERIENCE

STUDENT NAME: HARRISON THORPE

Program Choice: Camp Bighorn Journey is an 8-month gap year program that focuses on adventure and pushing your adventure level to the limit while getting a deep connection to God, deeper than you could imagine. (https://www.campbighorn.com/adventures/journey)

What do you hope to learn from your gap season? I hope to learn more about myself and how to push myself to be a better man, to get to my own goals, and to grow as a man of God with the skills I can use over the rest of my life.

Potential Career Pathway: I hope to get a clearer idea for my future, but I hope to have my own company with a few backup options just in case. I hope to explore being an entrepreneur of some sort or general contractor.

Decision Maker: I made this decision because I want to get my life started and I need to take it step-by-step. Also, my bucket list since I was young was to be financially stable enough to have a wife and kids and to grow up a real man. This program is helping me be more vulnerable yet strong.

Benefits: A new start, as well as time to reflect and grow faster than ever before. I have connected with Jesus and other people like I never would have expected and grew so much faster now that I'm away from home and with a different type of people.

Drawbacks: At first, leaving my family for several months and being many hours away for the first time and seeing people that I have never met or talked to in my life, but now I can honestly say nothing at all.

What would you tell upcoming students about how to decide what to do after high school? College is worthless unless you already know what you want to do and unless what you want to do requires a degree. A gap year will help clear your mind to focus on what you need to focus on while taking a break from the 12 years of hard schoolwork. You learn so much more about yourself and others and I believe that's what'll help you the most in the long run.

Anything Else? I'm so excited I chose this option. I feel like an entirely new person and I'm so ready to start my life. I understand how deciding can be very nerve-wracking for many reasons which is why you need to focus on the main goal of building the life you want for yourself.

STUDENT EXPERIENCE

STUDENT NAME: MADISON SINNOTT

Program Choice: YWAM (Youth With A Mission) 6-month discipleship training program, 3 months of training by lectures, and 3 months of outreach. I am doing both lecture and outreach in Hawaii on the Big Island. (https://www.ywamshipskona.org)

What do you hope to learn from their gap season? I learned about the character and nature of God and how he interacts with us. We have learned things like how he speaks to us, what he has done and what he is doing, and what our role is in the relationship with him, all these things are taught alongside the Bible in addition to applying this towards evangelism and learning how to preach the gospel effectively.

Potential Career Pathway: I am considering either staying with YWAM and staffing a school like the one I am in now, or I will go back home and go to college to become a high school teacher.

Benefits: I am learning how to build a firm foundation through the Lord and his word that will help me throughout the rest of my life. I am also learning so much about my identity in the Lord and who he is.

Drawbacks: Honestly, this has been one of the best decisions I could have ever made. The only hard part has been being away from home and my family and friends, especially my little brother.

What would you tell upcoming students about how to decide what to do after high school? As amazing as college is, it's not always the only option. Be open to exploring what else is available to you.

Anything Else? Listen to what you want, not what others want for you. Do your research and be informed, but make your decision based on what you want to do.

GAP SEASON CASE STUDIES

PARENT EXPERIENCE

*Note: parents listed may not be related
to students mentioned above*

PARENT NAME: ELLEN THORPE

Program Choice: Journey Program in Montana. This gap year program is for ages 18-26. They accept 12 students each year and it runs just like the school year. Journey is a safe space where participants are encouraged to ask hard questions and wrestle with doubts. Participants will spend time with mature Christians, learning how to read the Bible for themselves, establish Biblical foundations, and understand God's unconditional love in deeper ways. Discipleship is a primary focus, and Journey students will leave the program knowing how to talk about their faith and teach others to follow Jesus as well. https://www.campbighorn. com/adventures/journey

What does your teen hope to learn from their gap season? A clearer vision for his next step in life, more direction. A better understanding of his strengths and options.

Potential Career Pathway: So far, he is strongly considering a career in building/construction. He is talking about training for Express Sunrooms and opening a franchise somewhere in the southeast.

How did you help your teen with their decision?
When Harrison said he wanted to possibly do a gap year, we told him to do his homework and come to us once he figured out some ideas. Once he did that, he had narrowed it down to two options. We helped him look deeper into this, did more research, talked with the program's directors, looked at reviews. It was through this process that he was able to choose the best program for himself.

Benefits: Meeting one on one with his mentor has been extremely helpful. Having time alone with God to pray specifically for things on his mind and being quiet enough to hear what God is saying to him. Doing adventures like rock climbing, white water kayaking, hiking, things he has little to no experience in, has shown him how capable he is, giving him confidence.

Drawbacks: On our end, it's so far from home that getting him there and home is not easy

What would you tell parents about how to help their students decide what to do after high school? I would say to be open to this option and do your homework because there are many pro- grams like this available! Look for ones your stu- dent would grow from but also where they would be excited about! Let them take ownership of the process, let them have some skin in the game. Be supportive of their choice and guide them by asking questions they may not be thinking of: ques- tions about what they hope to gain in the follow- ing year, what is most important to them, and what their short and long term goals are and then look at every option they can think of, and talk about the pros and cons of each.

Anything Else? I spent his entire senior year worrying about his future. What if he didn't go to college? How would he ever get a job? How would he ever support himself or a family? Would he regret it? I fretted and worried myself sick! All that time was wasted though because he, in his choice, is doing so well! I regret all the days I gave to worry instead of trusting in God's perfect plan for Harrison.

GAP SEASON CASE STUDIES

PARENT EXPERIENCE

PARENT NAME: ALLI BRADLEY

Program Choice: Still working on it but traveling/ training for future work in the travel/hospitality industry.

Potential Career Pathway: Travel/Hospitality. She has the ultimate dream of sailing in the Caribbean with families and training them to scuba dive and helping them with their adventures.

How did you help your teen with their decision? I hired Stephanie to help her process and develop a plan to pursue her dream.

Benefits: She is free to dream about anything she wants to do...

Drawbacks: There are a lot of options, so it is difficult for her to narrow down what to do first.

What would you tell parents about how to help their students decide what to do after high school? I would encourage parents to work with a life coach to help navigate their student's plans if college is not in the books. It can be easy to fall into a "rut"-she could stay here and wait tables and make plenty of money, but it wouldn't be what her dreams are...

Anything Else? Even though she is now an adult, I have been helping her navigate all of the options... she wants to do it all on her own as she is a "grown up"-but also a lot of things to consider and think about-we talk about it often and research together.

WHEN COLLEGE IS RIGHT
IT WORKS

Julie* knows she wants to go to college, but she's not sure why, or even which one, or what to do once she's there. While everyone in her family has gone to college and there is an expectation she will too, she struggles to feel excited or even the desire to plan.

In our sessions together we focused first on her passions and values to determine a potential career pathway. From there we focused on looking at all the options available to her to make sure this option was her best fit. Once she determined it was, her excitement began to grow, and she was ready to plan. We dove in next to creating a list of criteria (majors, locations, costs, etc.) and began researching the potential schools that fit her criteria. It became clear to her that she had several viable options. We discussed that applying to a school did not require her to go there should

* not their real names

she get accepted (a common misconception among teens) and so she determined to apply to all of them. She was accepted to her top two, went and visited each and talked with her program advisor, and happily chose a particular school that was her best fit. As a result of her careful research and planning according to her career path, she has loved every minute of her experience and is gaining the learning she needs to step into any number of careers within her career path.

Personally, my chosen career path required a college education. From the time I was in second grade, I knew I wanted to be a teacher and so there was no better option for me. While I could have attended our local community college, I was also itching to leave my hometown and "spread my wings." I did the research and chose a school that had the best teacher certification program at the time (thank you CSU Chico!) and set off. Five years later I had a California Certified Secondary Education Teaching Credential, a bachelor's degree in English, and a job as a high school teacher. I had achieved the success I wanted based on the career I wanted to go into.

While not everyone is cut out for a 4-year college education, those who are can experience great success when they plan their collegiate experience with the end in mind.

Universities and colleges can offer fantastic opportunities for today's high school graduates. Supporters point out that having a degree means more open doors in the future, whether a graduate works in that degree area or not.

There are also the added financial earning opportunities a college degree has. According to a 2019 CNN Business article written by Anna Bahney of CNN Business:[20] "The average college graduate earns $78,000 a year compared to the $45,000 earned by someone with only a high school education, according to the analysis. That's a 75% premium, or more than $30,000 a year."

Additionally, there are the social and networking benefits of college. College students can meet people who may become network influencers, interact with leading researchers and experts in their fields, or even participate in ground-breaking studies that could change the way we live.

For those students wishing to pursue athletics beyond high school, 4-year colleges offer the best opportunity, especially for women for whom professional sports teams are less common. Whether at a community or 4-year college, athletes who are not at least enrolled for a minimum of one year are usually not eligible to pursue their sport professionally (there are exceptions, of course).

Last, some careers require a college degree, whether that be a Bachelor's, Master's, or Ph.D. and so a college education becomes a gateway through which your teenager can enter their chosen career path. For doctors, lawyers, counselors, researchers, and educators (to name a few professions), a 4-year college degree is essential.

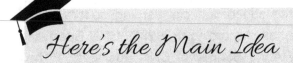

Here's the Main Idea

While not everyone is cut out for a 4-year college education, those who are can experience great success when they plan their collegiate experience with the end in mind.

Academically, colleges strive to offer a top-notch experience that both prepares their graduates for their chosen profession and expands their thinking beyond what they grew up with. Many colleges are on the cutting-edge of new technologies and research that students can participate in. They are also given the opportunity to develop their own ground-breaking research and interact with leaders from all industry areas both in the classroom and in the field. Most colleges require internships for graduation and many also offer study abroad programs, further adding to a student's academic development. Multiple opportunities also exist for students to explore concentrations of studies and potential careers they may never have thought of.

Aside from academics, colleges help ensure their students have the best experience possible away from home. From Freshman Mentors, to Family Weekends, to offering a club or organization for almost every interest, college can be a fantastic way for our teens to get and remain connected. Adding the benefits of familiar fast-food chains and on-campus personal services such as salons, massages, and even clothing stores, can all help teens be as comfortable as possible as they adjust to life away from home. Services for academics, counseling (personal and career), and advising are all established to ensure our kids can have the best possible experience in these formative years.

Attending a 4-year college after high school graduation can have emotional benefits as well. Bonding through the first-year experience away from home and all things familiar, experiencing the camaraderie of a fraternity or sorority, navigating current social and cultural issues as part of a club or organization, learning to live with roommates, and even experiencing classes with people different from their norm can all help today's teen grow beyond academics.

Last, taking the time between high school graduation and the early 20's to continue their education can allow teens to enter into the real world more slowly, allowing them to ease into adulthood.

There are downsides to this option as well. As the need for degrees has risen, so too the competitiveness of the application process and college attendance costs. It is no longer possible to get into most colleges without a cumulative GPA of at least a 3.0 (for some, the minimum is now a 4.0), ACT/SAT scores that rank at least as high as the previous year's average scores (with higher being better), and even additional acceptance into programs that may be impacted due to high interest.

The cost of college has skyrocketed due to rising popularity, further hindering many of today's students from being able to attend unless they are willing to put themselves into tens of thousands of dollars (or more) of debt. Parents who want to help their teens financially are often trying to save money in college planning accounts while also trying to afford their own cost of living, which creates its own set of questions: Are parents responsible for providing for their teen's education once they are adults? Is incurring personal debt to pay for their teen's education appropriate?

Every parent wants their child to succeed in life, but the 4-year college presents a whole host of concerns: Is the stress of trying to measure up in high school to be qualified to apply worth it? Do the social aspects of college outweigh the educational aspects? Does attending college prepare teens for real life? Is this the best opportunity based on the return of the investment of time and money?

It is important for parents and teens both to weigh the benefits and drawbacks of attending a 4-year college right after high school. **To determine if this option is the best path for your teen, consider the following:**

 Is your teenager interested in attending college right after high school? Too often, well-meaning parents encourage their teens to pursue a 4-year college degree without really assessing their desire. The family legacy focus assumes a teenager will attend the school everyone in their family did, adding an additional layer of pressure. High schools also inadvertently add the pressure to conform as they announce with pride at each Senior Night and graduation ceremony the prestigious universities and 4-year colleges their graduates are attending. Teens who are pressured into attending a 4-year college when they aren't ready or interested do not do well. Have you asked your teen whether they want to attend a 4-year college right after high school? Do they believe they have any other choice?

 Is your teenager emotionally ready to go off to college right after high school? We have all heard the stories of teens who fail out after their first semester due to too much partying, or those who become so anxious about succeeding they leave within weeks of the start of a term. It is important to help your teenager assess their emotional maturity. Not being ready emotionally can result in the loss of thousands of dollars of tuition and housing, scholarships, and even sports eligibility (for collegiate athletes). Will your teen be able to handle the freedom they will experience, the multitude of different cultures, and not being close to family and friends? Will they be able to handle budgeting both time and finances? Is your teen ready to be fully responsible for planning their education since parents are no longer included in the experience?

Is your teenager (or you) prepared to pay for their degree? According to a 2019 article written by Jaleesa Bustamante on the research done by EducationData.org,[21] the average cost of a 4-year degree is approximately $122,000. That is if a student graduates in 4 years which, according to the same data, only 39% of students do, while a full 60% take 6 years to earn a degree. This does not consider in-state vs out-of state tuition costs, which can have substantial differences, or even travel costs to and from college. Do you have a financial plan, or a plan to develop one, that helps your teen understand and accept their financial responsibilities of this option? Are they willing to do so?

 Is your teenager interested in a career for which a 4-year college degree is essential? There are some programs of study that begin the freshman year. Athletic training programs, for example, require students to begin in the fresh-man year, so transferring from a community college would be a detriment. Education students are often enrolled in specialized classes in the first year as well. If your teen is interested in a career that requires a 4-year degree, it would be beneficial to research the program of studies at the schools they are interested in. If not, a plan that includes other options like transferring from a community college may be more beneficial.

Has your teen determined the career pathway they want to take and whether a full 4-year college degree is required?

 Is your teenager interested in becoming a collegiate athlete? Teens who wish to pursue their sport beyond high school are often limited to the experience colleges offer. While club sports and community colleges are viable options, should your teen wish to cover college costs with athletic scholarships or is interested in pursuing a career as a professional athlete, a 4-year college may be their only option. This option has a multitude of additional steps and costs, however. Social media engagement, recruiting combines and camps, contacting coaches and participating in their recruiting process, and spending time developing stats sheets and highlight videos are all part of the process to become eligible to be recruited and hopefully given an offer. The time investment alone is roughly equivalent to a semi-full-time job. Is your teen ready to engage in what it will take? Check out the National Collegiate Athletic Association (NCAA)[22] and organizations such as Next College Student Athlete (NCSA)[23] for more on the recruiting process.

 Is your teenager willing to compete for scholarships? There are multitudes of scholarships available to help teens pay for college. Some are based on test scores, cumulative GPA's, and class ranks. Others often require high school students to compete, spending countless hours on essays, projects, interviews, etc. to be considered. Making the time to participate in this process can be tough for today's involved high school students. Is your teenager interested in achieving the grades and scores necessary to qualify? Does your teen have the time to apply for scholarships to financially contribute to the costs of their education?

 Is your teenager willing to start their career in debt if needed? Filling out the FAFSA form is the gateway to government aid as well as loans. While grants do not have to be paid back, loans do. They are attractive because they do not have to be paid until a student graduates, but will the amount of debt your teen accrues be able to be paid off by the career they plan to pursue? Would there be a financial benefit to attending a community college first, or enrolling in a trade or certification program to save money and lessen the amount of debt? Many adults incur tens of thousands of dollars of debt in a career that will not support repayment. Is your teen's current career choice able to support repayment of any necessary loans? (For more on this including a student debt calculator, check out the Next Steps Guide.)

Has your teenager determined a career cluster? College is too expensive to just wander through. Having a clearly defined career cluster is not a limitation, but rather helps teens focus when making class selections and determining a major. While majors may change, there is a greater chance a student will graduate within both a reasonable amount of time and their financial budget when they pursue a degree that represents a series of clearly identified potential careers within a particular career cluster. Has your teenager identified a specific career cluster they want to pursue? If not, take the time before your teen pays that acceptance deposit to develop at least a particular cluster area to focus on. (For more on this, see the Next Steps section at the end of this book.)

When pursuing a college degree right after high school is the right fit for your teenager everyone wins. The key is making sure your teen has carefully planned out their career pathway, determined a college degree is required, and is ready for the experience.

4-YEAR COLLEGE CASE STUDIES

STUDENT EXPERIENCE

STUDENT NAME: KELSEY TOTTY

School Choice: Mississippi State University

Program Choice: Master of Sport Administration

Potential Career Pathway: Athletics - uncertain on which exact field of it.

Decision Maker: I fell in love with working with the football team in high school when I saw how my efforts were benefiting the team.

Benefits: While in my undergraduate studies, the material clicked for me, and my love for working in the sports industry has only grown. I have no regrets about the career path I have chosen.

Drawbacks: The job market for sports is highly competitive and difficult to get into.

What would you tell upcoming students about how to decide what to do after high school? Find something you love, if you get to school and find out that it might not be what is best for you, then change to something that brings you joy. There is nothing wrong with changing your mind, this is something you will potentially do for the rest of your life.

Anything Else? College is not always the right path for everyone, it is okay to decide to do something else. If you do decide to go to college, go somewhere that feels like home, you will know it when you get there.

4-YEAR COLLEGE CASE STUDIES

STUDENT EXPERIENCE

STUDENT NAME: MIA TUBBIOLO

School Choice: Winthrop University

Program Choice: I started with Psychology but changed to Social Work

Potential Career Pathway: Therapist of some sort

Decision Maker: I've always wanted to help people and think mental health is especially important.

Benefits: Getting a new experience out of my hometown and taking classes I am interested in.

Drawbacks: Trying to decide whether I want to go to college.

What would you tell upcoming students about how to decide what to do after high school? Do what you think is best for your future not what you think is right (based on what everyone else is doing) or "normal."

Anything Else? I picked college as my pathway for after high school because I already had an idea of what I wanted to do. I don't know if I would have chosen college if I had no idea.

4-YEAR COLLEGE CASE STUDIES

PARENT EXPERIENCE

*Note: parents listed may not be related
to students mentioned above*

PARENT NAME: KRISTI TOTTY (Child #1)

School Choice: Mississippi State University

Program Choice: Master of Sport Administration

Potential Career Pathway: Sports Administration
- specifically Athletic Academics

How did you help your teen with their decision?
I had lots of conversations with her, helped her to
explore degree options and we attended school
visits together.

Benefits: She still has a passion for her field (she
is now earning her Master's) and has found a
specialty she loves within the broad pathway she
started with.

Drawbacks: It's hard to find quality internships.

What would you tell parents about how to help their students decide what to do after high school? Help your student identify (for themselves) what their talents and passions are; don't put them in a box of your assumptions and perceptions. Brainstorm and explore with them.

4-YEAR COLLEGE CASE STUDIES

PARENT EXPERIENCE

PARENT NAME: LORIN TINDER

School Choice: College of Charleston

Program Choice:
Anthropology (Bachelor of Science degree)

Potential Career Pathway:
something in Environmental Science possibly

How did you help your teen with their decision?
She liked the English and History classes she experienced in high school and decided it was interesting. It was also a subject in which she excelled.

Benefits: It's opened her eyes to other cultures and how our environment affects our own culture and lifestyles.

Drawbacks: If she wanted to pursue Anthropology alone the job possibilities are narrower, and she has to have a doctorate to teach or make any big money.

What would you tell parents about how to help their students decide what to do after high school? If they are not sure what they want to do they should take a gap year and work in a field they think they might be interested in to see if it's a good fit. Or pick a major that has an overly broad range of possibilities for jobs - like business or communications or one of the sciences if possible. I just happened to have a student strong in English and History. I wish I had pushed harder for her to get career counseling or planning.

4-YEAR COLLEGE CASE STUDIES

PARENT EXPERIENCE

PARENT NAME: PAIGE HOWELL (Child #2)

School Choice: University of South Carolina

Program Choice: Business

Potential Career Pathway: Business but not sure. His degree is pretty broad.

How did you help your teen with their decision? Conversations, research, and monetary support.

Benefits:
He has had time to explore different options.

Drawbacks: I don't think he was ready for a 4-year college, especially with virtual learning.

What would you tell parents about how to help their students decide what to do after high school? Begin the discussion early so that they give themselves options.

COLLEGIATE ATHLETICS CASE STUDIES

STUDENT EXPERIENCE

STUDENT NAME: CHRISTOPHER HAYNES

School Choice:
Johnson and Wales University, Charlotte

Sport: Men's Soccer

Program Choice:
Sports Entertainment and Event Management

What was the recruiting process like for you?
The best way I can describe my recruiting process would be laborious. A lot of the difficulties were self-inflicted, however. I found that the more fearful you are the cloudier your path becomes.

What is your end goal of being a collegiate athlete? If I'm honest, I'm not sure.

Potential Career Pathway: Sports Management

Decision Maker: Location, coach, available degrees. I followed what I was passionate about. I chose what I thought was going to make me the happiest and give me the best chance of success.

Benefits: I've dug into myself through this whole process and I've uncovered more in these past few years than I have in my entire life. The answers I've gotten have been the most beneficial aspect.

Drawbacks: The biggest drawback has been that I've become unsure of who I'm supposed to be or what I'm supposed to do with everything going on around me (school, soccer, friends).

What would you tell upcoming students about how to decide what to do after high school? I would say to follow what you love, even if you feel like there's a chance that you might fail. Avoiding taking chances due to fear of rejection is something I've always struggled with and I know many people who struggle with the same thing. As cliché as it is, a leap of faith is sometimes where you find your grounding and truly discover who you are supposed to be.

Anything Else? My final piece of advice would be to not let setbacks and failures ruin your mindset. Sometimes the best way to move forward is to take a step back and focus on what YOU want.

COLLEGIATE ATHLETICS CASE STUDIES

STUDENT EXPERIENCE

STUDENT NAME: SAM HARTMAN

School Choice: Wake Forest University

Sport: Football

What was the recruiting process like for you?
It was easy because I committed early.

Potential Career Pathway:
I want to play at the next level (NFL)

Decision Maker: I didn't choose this life, it chose me. But I also knew Wake was a great school. I liked the location and the culture of the locker room and was able to experience it during recruiting visits.

Benefits: The friendships and bonds I've made with my teammates. I've had the opportunity to play in different stadiums around the country, i.e., Yankee Stadium for a bowl game, which is an awesome experience.

Drawbacks: There have been no drawbacks; it's everything I expected and more.

What would you tell upcoming students about how to decide what to do after high school? For students who are interested in playing a sport in college- don't make your decision on anything that could change, i.e., coaching staff. Choose the school, its size, or its culture. Make the decision your choice, not your parents'. Spend time at the school, around the team. Ask current students/student-athletes about the school and its culture-get the brutal truth.

Anything Else? Being close to home is nice, it's not lame. Being able to go home for a day or a week-end is a big advantage. If you don't love football (or whatever your sport) don't try to get a scholarship or play in college. It's like a job; and if you don't love it, you'll hate it. It goes by fast, enjoy every moment and appreciate the friendships you make. Those guys will be with you in the good times and bad, during college, and for the rest of your life.

COLLEGIATE ATHLETICS CASE STUDIES

PARENT EXPERIENCE

*Note: parents listed may not be related
to students mentioned above*

PARENT NAME: LISA HARTMAN

School Choice: Wake Forrest

Sport: Football

What were the determining factors for your teen to play a sport? The education he would receive at Wake combined with playing football at a Power 5 program.

Potential Career Pathway: He would like to play in the NFL.

What was the recruiting process like for you? This was our second son to go through the recruiting process, so having the previous exposure (obviously) made it so much easier. Also, Sam verbally committed to Wake super early, with just a couple of other offers, his sophomore year of high school. He never entertained conversations from other schools or coaches, so didn't deal with that "car salesman" talk!

How did you help your teen with their decision? We emphasized hard work and dedication to be good enough to play in college, especially at a Power 5 school. As a family, we made it a priority to put practice, workouts, extra training, or anything to help his journey first-before vacations or family events. If Sam was committed to being his best, we all were committed to helping him get there. (This was the same with all 3 boys.)

Benefits: Knowing he has the whole community of football-teammates, coaches, academic support, etc. helping and watching out for his best interest. It's like having an instant "family" as soon as you enroll.

Drawbacks: I haven't found a drawback yet. (he is a Junior)

What would you tell parents about how to help their students decide what to do after high school? If he/she wants to play a sport, they need to be willing to work hard to do all the little extra things to make you the best player you can be - nutrition, sleep, practice and cross-train. Also, D2, D3 schools can be awesome and I wouldn't rule them out. Joe went to a D3 school with an incredible academic reputation and played basketball.

Having the instant "family" made the transition so much easier for both him and his parents to leave him 8 hours from home.

Anything Else? I'm so grateful our boys played sports through school. It has helped with time management, organization, and being exposed to so many different people and experiences. They stayed busy and out of trouble (!) and it created a healthy lifestyle that they will hopefully keep throughout their life.

COLLEGIATE ATHLETICS CASE STUDIES

STUDENT EXPERIENCE

PARENT NAME: KRISTI TOTTY (Child #2)

School Choice:
Knox College (2 yr.), now Columbia College

Sport: Soccer and Football

What were the determining factors for your teen to play a sport? The quality of education and certain degrees offered; the success of the soccer program; the proximity to home.

Potential Career Pathway: To play professionally in the European league.

What was the recruiting process like for you? Being the mom/female (divorced from his dad), I was not included in the recruiting process.

How did you help your teen with their decision? I offered unconditional support and didn't complain about not being part of the process.

Benefits: Exposure to other cultures and introduction to "adulting"

Drawbacks: He has not loved the courses he has taken. He is struggling to find clarity and a pathway to thrive in.

What would you tell parents about how to help their students decide what to do after high school? Help your student identify (for themselves) their strengths and passions.

Anything Else? If divorced, have a plan ahead of time for how you will co-parent these decisions - not just a custody agreement from the settlement ...there is so much more than just who pays for what.

PART THREE
THE NEXT STEPS GUIDE

NEXT STEPS
STARTING POINT

This section includes specific conversation opportunities you can engage in with your teenager to help them identify and pursue their best pathway to success after high school. Don't just jump into these conversations with your teen, however. There is a methodology and a mindset that will help give your teen the best opportunity at a successful life after high school.

THE METHODOLOGY

1. **Examine your expectations.** We all have high hopes for our children, but those can often become expectations that are unhealthy. Do you have a particular route in mind you expect your teen to take? Are you willing to be flexible

and accept a different decision? Do you believe your teen should have a clear decision and be actively pursuing it? Answers to these questions can often create tension between parents and their teens which can make having any kind of conversation about their future a major argument. Commit to allowing your teen to explore and determine for themselves, with your guidance, what might be the best post-high school option or options for them without telling them what you think they need to do. Then discuss their choices. At this stage, teens need time to process and explore, and to know they will not disappoint their parents with their choices. Teens are overwhelmed, afraid of missing out, and are struggling to make a decision. They need support and encouragement to explore.

2. **Beware of comparison.** One of the biggest barriers to a healthy conversation is comparison. No one wants to admit they believe their child to not be good enough, but we can fall into that trap when they do not measure up to our expectations, other siblings, or our friend's children. Identifying that limiting belief and determining to not compare your teenager to anyone else and expressing this to your teen, will help you listen to them with an open mind and help them trust you enough to open up.

3. **Be clear about your involvement in their future.** Be prepared to share how much (if any) you have to offer them financially, how long you will support their living at home, how long they can go without a plan, and any other boundaries you want to set. This will help your teenager make well-informed decisions.

4. **Create an environment of trust.** Make sure your teen knows you are willing to support any well thought out decision they make. Our children want to make us proud and are aware they may disappoint us if they choose something we don't like. Help your teen know you want to help them figure out what is best for them and that you will trust their choice. Keep in mind "support" does not mean "pay for" or "without boundaries." Building trust includes telling your teenager what support from you does and does not look like.

5. **Give your teen the gift of time.** A decision about their future cannot be made in one conversation. It often takes multiple conversations, over months and even years, before a teen can be clear enough to decide. This is to be expected and even encouraged. Today's teenagers have more time than we allow them and the pressure to get things done now only adds to their already huge anxiety over deciding. Set up a series of consistent "conversation meetings" where you prepare your teen beforehand with the questions

you want to discuss so they have time to prepare their answers. Teenagers often need time to process and giving them time to do this before hand may produce more productive conversations.

THE MINDSET

Our teenagers can become fearful of making a mistake, disappointing us, and missing out on something important. They spend a majority of their days in school where, if they do not fit the model of the average student at their school, they either feel bored because they are not challenged and begin to "tune out", or they come to believe they are not smart enough because they can't keep up. For those students who do fit the mold, there can be constant striving to keep up to make sure they fit, or a complete rejection and possible shutdown. The result is a feeling of being stuck that begins to breed negative thoughts that impact our teenager's ability to believe their dreams are possible.

This occurs over time, almost imperceptibly, and yet, as their parents, we can sense it. Our once ambitious child who wanted to be an astronaut or ballerina or firefighter is now seemingly without a clue of what to do with their life as they near high school graduation. They have now come to believe they are not capable, or even worthy, of pursuing their dreams. As parents, we feel helpless. We want to inspire and encourage our teens, but all our efforts seem to be met with slammed doors and emotional resistance. It is a tough place to be for everyone.

When teenagers get to a place where they struggle to believe in their ability to change or even achieve, they are considered to have a fixed mindset. A fixed mindset believes things are the way they are, and nothing can change them. According to an article by Gregory Ciotti on the Sparring Mind website,[24] a fixed mindset "assume[s] intelligence, character, and creative potential are unchangeable attributes writ in stone since birth-that they cannot be modified in a meaningful way." What this means is that our teenagers can develop a belief that there is no way they can change or achieve their dreams; that if they are behind in school, they always will be and won't be able to handle college, so why try; that if they aren't smart now because their grades do not tell them they are, they never will be.

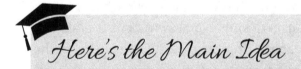

Here's the Main Idea

A fixed mindset believes things are the way they are, and nothing can change them. A growth mindset believes that failures, challenges, and obstacles are temporary; that each option can become an experiment in learning.

I believe we are not born with a fixed mindset but develop it over time as we experience inevitable failure, setback, and struggle. A fixed mindset develops when we come to believe our failures are markers of our abilities, rather than opportunities to learn. For example, a student who struggles early in math begins to speak phrases like "I am no good at math" or "I'll never be able to do well in math." As they speak these limitations, they come to believe them, "fixing" in their minds a false belief that their math ability can never improve or even that their lack of ability means they are a failure (especially for high achieving students who believe an A is the only worthy grade). For a student, this mindset is catastrophic because it limits their desire and even the ability to dream about what could be.

Dr. Caroline Leaf, in her book, *Think, Learn, Succeed*[25] explains that speaking and believing negative ideas about ourselves, our abilities, and our world, creates physical neural pathways in the brain that eventually become habitual patterns of thought. Think of it like this: what we think over and over begins to form expressways in our brain that bypass other thoughts. The more we think something the more that thought becomes automatic and travels on that expressway with less and less conscious processing. In the case of a student who struggles in math, the more they speak that they are not good at math, the more they believe it. The more they believe it the less likely they become to attempt to learn and grow, as the "expressway" of "poor in math" becomes an automatic and unconscious thought. The same is true with any other thought we repeat over and over.

The good news is that we can demolish those limiting mindset expressways and create new growth mindset-based ones instead.

A growth mindset believes that failures, challenges, and obstacles are temporary; that each opportunity can become an experiment in learning. The most important reason I believe as to why teenagers are stymied in developing a growth mindset concerning their educational abilities, and therefore their belief about the possibilities available to them in their future, comes in the assigning of grades as a measure of achievement, effort, and success. I understand why grades are necessary, but when grades become the only or most important marker of a students' success, they no longer feel safe to experiment and try, fearing that any deviance from what the teacher wants will result in a failing grade. And, thanks to our current culture, not having all A's and B's is seen as a failure to have a real chance at success in life.

So how do we help our teenagers develop a growth mindset? The same way negative expressways of thought are created: we help them speak positivity, opportunity, and hope into their lives, and speak it over them consistently. A teenager who says "I'll never be good at math" really means they are struggling and don't know how to meet the expectations they believe are necessary to succeed. Parents can help their teens by speaking possibility: "I know this math seems hard right now. What do you think you need to figure this out?" or "This math unit is hard, but you can still learn. Let's go back to the beginning."

What does this do for our kids? It helps them see you believe in them and that growth is possible. What does it do in their brains? Dr. Leaf's research has shown that the more a person works to turn a new thought into a habitual one (a process that takes about 63 days) they change the physical makeup of their brain and form new neural pathways of thought that replace the old expressways with new ones.

This. Is. Huge.

Parents, teachers, other adults, and students themselves can develop a growth mindset and therefore free the brain to believe anything is possible. The realists among us want to believe there are limitations, that not everything is possible. However, that is not up to us to declare over anyone else's life. If we choose to believe it for ourselves, that's one thing, but to influence a teen to believe there are limitations on their lives feeds into the same mentality that gets them stuck so that when it comes time to dream about their future they are overwhelmed by fear and see only limitations.

If your teenager is struggling with a fixed mindset, here are a few ways you can help them develop a growth mindset instead:

1. Have a conversation about the differences between a fixed and growth mindset. (A simple Google search will even provide images and phrases to use.) Most teens have no idea what a mindset is, let alone whether they have a fixed or growth one.

2. Ask your teen which mindset they believe they have and how they arrived at that conclusion.

3. Have your teen compare the emotional effects of each mindset. Start with an area they are currently struggling in. Have them speak their limitations and fears out loud and ask them how that makes them feel. Next, have them re-word their struggle in growth mindset terms and ask them how they feel and what differences they notice between the two approaches to the same struggle.

4. Ask your teen how their mental attitude about the possibilities of their future would shift if they developed a stronger growth mindset.

5. Ask your teen to make a list of at least five beliefs they currently say to themselves about their education abilities (refer to the math example above). Have them identify which beliefs are of a fixed mindset and which are of a growth mindset. Then, have them reword the fixed mindset phrases into growth mindset ones and practice saying those aloud instead of the fixed mindset ones.

Here's the Main Idea

Parents, teachers, other adults and students themselves can develop a growth mindset and therefore free the brain to believe anything is possible.

Developing a growth mindset takes time, patience, and diligence, but it can be done. If your teenager is struggling, as their parent you have tremendous power. Keep speaking the limitlessness of their potential. Keep reminding them they have tremendous value to add to our society. Keep telling them over, and over, and over, and over that their uniqueness has a significant place in this world. When adults speak possibility over children, we help shape their growth mindset, unleashing them to dream and develop the courage they will need to make a difference in our world.

When we can help teenagers develop a growth mindset about their future, a world of opportunities opens up for them, creating a safer place from which to dream about what could be without fearing the repercussions of potential failures based on their current mistakes.

Make the time to work through this methodology and mindset development before you move to the conversations about which option to pursue after high school. Doing so will make those conversations much smoother.

NO CLUE? NO PROBLEM!
START HERE

*If your teen is struggling without any
idea where to start, begin here.*

Often, a teenager who doesn't know what to do needs help aligning to what's most important to them. This section of conversations can help your teen identify what is most important to them and allow them to see their future from that perspective.

Set up a series of no-pressure conversations to work through the following questions as appropriate for your teen, allowing them to tell you their thoughts and perspectives. Do your best to create a safe space and be patient with your teen and yourself. This may all be new and will take time.

Remember, our role is to serve as a guide to help them identify what is most important. Feel free to customize each conversation for your teen.

QUESTIONS TO IDENTIFY PERSONAL VALUES

1. How would you rank the following in order of importance according to what you couldn't live without (least important being 9 and most important being 1)?

    a. Faith

    b. Family (current)

    c. Friends

    d. Money

    e. Meaningful Career

    f. Marriage

    g. Prestige among colleagues or friends

    h. Notoriety/Fame within your career

    i. Children of your own

2. Is there anything else you would list as valuable to you?

3. What influenced your ranking?

4. What do you currently spend most of your time doing each day?

5. How does that activity reflect what's most important to you?

6. How do you define success?

7. What factors are most important to you when you think about success for yourself?

8. If you had no limit to anything you could do to be successful in life, what would you choose to do? What about this excites you the most? What about this idea scares you the most?

QUESTIONS TO IDENTIFY PASSION POINTS

1. How do you define passion (specifically related to the purpose of daily living)?

2. What causes, groups, philosophies, and/or events get you the most fired up that something must change? What specific change(s) do you want to see?

3. If you could change one thing in the world, what would it be? How would you change it? What do you hope would happen because of the changes you would make?

4. When you imagine the world you want to live in as an adult, what do you hope it is like? Be as specific as possible, considering governments and their influence on the populace, how people treat one another, finances, technology, transportation, housing, education, etc.

5. What would you be willing to do to make that dream world a reality?

6. What is one change you can start to make in the world around you today? What about that change is important to you?

7. What do you believe about the possibility that you can make significant changes in the world?

QUESTIONS AND RESOURCES TO UNCOVER POTENTIAL CAREER CLUSTER PATHWAYS

These questions are for your teen to think about and research. There are a lot of questions and there is a lot of information gathering. Your teen may do better if you work with them or on their own. Do what you think is best according to who they are.

1. Rank the following industry areas according to what seems most interesting to you to learn more about (1 is most important, 16 is least important).

   Note: If you do not know about these career pathways, consider using a Google search of each area to learn more.

   a. Agriculture, Food, and Natural Resources

   b. Architecture and Construction

   c. Arts, Audio/Video Technology, and Communications

   d. Business Management and Administration

   e. Education and Training

   f. Finance

   g. Government and Public Administration

   h. Health Science

    i.   Hospitality and Tourism

    j.   Human Services

    k.   Information Technology

    l.   Law, Public Safety, Corrections and Security

    m. Manufacturing

    n.   Marketing, Sales, and Service

    o.   Science, Technology, Engineering, and Mathematics

    p.   Transportation, Distribution, and Logistics

2. What about your most favorite choice seems the most interesting to you? How does that choice reflect your values and passions?

3. Have you ever done a career profile inventory "test"? If not, please consider taking one. There are three I have used:

    a.   Myers Briggs (free): https://www.16personalities.com/

    b.   Naviance (if your school doesn't have it there will be a fee): https://www.naviance.com/

    c.   In Charleston County you can use: https://www.charlestonempowered.com

4. What potential career options were you given?

5. For each career you are interested in (from your top career cluster or industry area), answer the following questions. I recommend using Google searches or this government site: https://www.bls.gov/careeroutlook/2015/article/career-clusters.html

    a. What are the potential career options of that career?

    b. Which seems the most interesting to you to learn more about? (*Note: if you know nothing about any of them you should learn a little more about all of them before answering.*)

    c. What education or certifications are required?

    d. If college is required, what major is associated with this career?

    e. How long does that training usually take?

    f. What is the expected potential income to start?

    g. What is the expected growth of this industry? (i.e., will there be more, or less, demand for this career in the future.)

6. Based on your research, what are the top 3 careers you are interested in?

PUTTING IT ALL TOGETHER

*Once your teenager has some
career ideas, continue here.*

Once your teen has a clear vision of what prospective careers they are interested in, the next step is to research all the potential pathways to that career available to them and determine what option(s) may fit them best. Depending on the career, a combination of several options may even be in order. For example, if a student is interested in film production, they might consider a gap season internship to learn more about the industry before considering the type of degree they want to pursue. Alternately, a student who knows what they want to do but needs more time to save up money for college might choose to work full-time, attend a community college first to save on costs, or even utilize the ROTC program or enlist in the armed services where their education can be paid for.

Parents can be extremely helpful in this part of the process. Teenagers often get overwhelmed, even when they are excited, because they do not know where to start or how to break down the task in front of them. Work with your teen to help them identify exactly what they hope to achieve, and then help them work backward from there to identify what steps need to be completed and when for them to be successful.

For example, if your teen decides they want to take a gap season to learn more about the career field they hope to enter, help them identify what they hope to achieve by the end of their gap season, and then brainstorm activities and create a timeline to follow to build a plan for a successful gap season experience.

There is no right way to enter a career which is why it is so beneficial for teenagers to explore all their options before choosing the one that's right for them. This section is meant to equip you to help your teen determine the best pathway or combination of pathways that may be the best fit for them. If your teen is unsure, I suggest looking at all the options. If they have a specific route they are interested in, I suggest having them focus on that first as a way of making sure it is the best fit for them. If it turns out that an option doesn't fit, you can guide them to moving on to exploring other options.

Most important, these discussions are not meant to be one conversation experiences. Each will take multiple conversations with time in between for processing and research. If your teen is older and time is short for deciding, you may want to pick and choose the best questions that will help them reach a decision within their time frame.

Each of the following option focus areas is meant for parents and their teens to do together, ideally by having a conversation using the open-ended questions. Your role is to guide your teen to their best option. The research is for them to complete as this is their future. They must want to develop their vision of a successful future more than you do. Offer honest answers to their questions about your thoughts and experience, and especially about your financial contribution, but allow your teenager to make their own decision.

No matter what, remember that there is no one-size-fits-all approach. Use whatever is here to help you in the way you think best for your teen.

HOW TO DETERMINE IF A COMMUNITY COLLEGE IS A GOOD FIT FOR YOU

 FOUNDATION QUESTIONS

- What most appeals to you about attending a 4-year college after high school?

- How did you arrive at this opinion?

- What benefits do you believe a 4-year college could provide for your future career ideas

- What drawbacks do you think this option would have for your future career?

 EXPLORATORY QUESTIONS

- What school(s) are you most interested in?

- What about this school/these schools appeals to you?

- What major(s) are you considering?

- If your teen has no idea:

  - Review the discussion questions from the first part of this Next Steps Guide to determine a particular career cluster area.

  - Using that career cluster area, have your teen research potential careers and the degrees and experience required (if necessary) for those careers.

  - Have your teen make a list of potential majors associated with the required degrees.

- What career(s) do you hope a degree in this area will lead to?

 RESEARCH QUESTIONS

- Have your teen look up each college they are interested in and answer the following questions:

- What majors and minors are offered by this college that can lead to a career in the career cluster you are interested in?

- What is the average length of time to achieve the needed degree at this school?

- What is the job placement rate for graduates of this school?

- What internship opportunities does this school provide?

- What does it cost to go to this school for the length of time you will need to earn your degree?

  - Tuition costs

  - Books/supplies/fees costs

  - Room and board costs (residence halls and apartment living)

  - Transportation costs

  - In-state tuition vs out-of-state tuition (if considering an out-of-state school, note how residency can be gained)

- How does this cost compare to what would be spent on general education units at a community college? (This may be especially helpful information for those seeking to attend an out-of-state school and need to establish residency.)

- What do you think about that cost difference?

FUTURE IMPLICATIONS QUESTIONS

In considering the costs of college there are several questions to reflect upon:

- How do you plan to pay for your education?

  - Parents: what part of your student's college education will you fund (if any, as this is not a requirement) and what they will have to fund is an important conversation.

- What is the average starting salary for the careers you are interested in?

- Will you have to take out loans to pay for this school?

- How would you rate the return on your investment in your future by attending this school?

- Will your student debt be able to be paid off by your career?

- How long will it take?

  - Consider researching student loan rates. The StudentAid.gov site (https://student aid.gov/understand-aid/types/loans interest-rates) lists the most up-to-date government loan rates. Also, check out your local banks for their rates and compare them.

  - Add your potential loan amount, interest rate, and length of time desired to pay it off into a debt calculator like this one from BankRate.com: https://www.bankrate. com/calculators/college-planning/loan-calculator.aspx

 ## FINAL REFLECTION QUESTIONS

As a final discussion, consider the following:

- What excites you the most about this option?

- What hesitations are you experiencing?

- How does this option differ from others you are considering?

FOR PARENTS

If you are funding all or part of your student's education, what boundaries do you need to establish for your student?

- Will you expect GPA minimums to remain in school?

- What happens if they fail a required class?

- If they are placed on academic probation, what will be your response?

- Will you financially reward your student for grades?

- Will you be paying for housing and personal expenses?

HOW TO DETERMINE IF A APPRENTICESHIP OR TRADE SCHOOL IS A GOOD FIT FOR YOU

 FOUNDATION QUESTIONS

- What are your initial thoughts about applying to a trade school or apprenticeship program before or after high school graduation?

- How did you arrive at this opinion?

- What benefits do you believe a trade school or apprenticeship program could provide for your future career ideas?

- What drawbacks do you think this option would have for your future career?

✿ RESEARCH QUESTIONS: TRADE SCHOOL

If no research has been done, have your teen Google (if needed) your local (or even out-of-state if that's a consideration) Trade school programs based on their career focus and select several to research. Then answer the following questions.

- What certifications does this option offer? (take the time to do a brief examination of each one)

- Which of these seems interesting to you to learn more about?

- How long will it take to complete the program?

- What are the application requirements for each program?

- What are the costs of each program?

- What is the job placement rate of each certificate program you are interested in?

- What is the career outlook for each certificate program you are interested in?

- What is the starting salary for each certificate program you are interested in?

**RESEARCH QUESTIONS:
APPRENTICESHIP PROGRAMS**

**Have your teen Google (if needed) your local
(or even out-of-state if that's a consideration)
Apprenticeship programs and select several
to research. Then answer the following
questions:**

*Note: Some youth apprenticeship programs can
start as early as 16 and as late as 18 (graduating
senior in high school). While there are adult
apprenticeship programs, this book focuses on
youth programs.*

**In South Carolina, there is the SC
Apprenticeship Program: http://www.
apprenticeshipcarolina.com/about.html**

**Once your teen has located available
programs in your area, have them
answer the following questions:**

- What industry areas are offered that you are
  interested in?

- What makes these areas interesting to you?

- What are the application requirements
  (including application deadlines)?

- What industry partners could you be working
  with?

- What income could you be making?

- What are the costs (if any) to participate?

- What is the career outlook for successful completion of the apprenticeships you are interested in?

✸ FUTURE IMPLICATIONS QUESTIONS

- How would you rate the return on your investment in your future by attending a trade school or enrolling in an apprenticeship program right after high school?

- If you choose either of these options, would you stay at home or rent an apartment?

If your teen chooses to stay at home (and is 18 or older):

- What changes do you think should be made to how we (parents) treat you while you live at home during this time?

- How will you treat our home as an adult?

- What are your thoughts about paying rent, paying your bills, and/ or earning your keep differently? (i.e., by helping with errands, younger siblings, household maintenance, etc.)

- What is your timeline for moving out on your own?

If your teen chooses to move out:

- What is your plan for how you will pay your rent, utilities, and bills?

- What research have you done about the cost of apartments near the schools you are interested in?

- How can you learn how much it will cost you to move out?

- What financial assistance do you think you will need from us? (if this is an option)

 FINAL REFLECTION QUESTIONS

As a final discussion, consider the following:

- What excites you the most about this/these options?

- What hesitations are you experiencing?

- How do this/these options differ from others you are considering?

HOW TO DETERMINE IF THE MILITARY IS A GOOD FIT FOR YOU

 FOUNDATION QUESTIONS

- What are your initial thoughts about joining the military after high school?

- How did you arrive at this opinion?

- What benefits do you believe the military could provide for your future career ideas?

- What drawbacks do you think this option would have for your future career?

 RESEARCH QUESTIONS

- What research have you done about the options available to you in the military?

If there has been no research, encourage your teen to spend time researching each option on one of the many sites online. (a few include: https://www.todaysmilitary.com/careers-benefits/explore-careers, and usa.gov/join-military)

Questions to encourage your teen to consider while researching:

- Which branch(es) of the military offer training for your potential future career aspiration?

- What does that training include?

- Who do you know in this/these branches that you could talk to?

- As much as is possible, try to help your teen arrange at least one interview with a veteran or active-duty member.

- Is there an ROTC option?

- What does that include?

- Which schools participate?

- How long would it take to receive all the training and education you would need to enter the career(s) you are interested in?

- How much of that would you have to pay for?

FUTURE IMPLICATIONS QUESTIONS

Once the research has been completed or if your teen has researched this option already, consider the following questions as part of a larger discussion about this option:

- What made you consider researching the military as an option for yourself?

- What branch are you considering?

- What benefits do you believe this option will have for you?

- How do you know?

- Who have you talked to about this?

- Arrange, if possible, for your teen to speak with at least one veteran or active-duty service member.

- What questions have you prepared for recruiters?

- If your teen hasn't prepared any questions, help them brainstorm. Being prepared to meet with recruiters is the best way to make sure your teen gets the information they need to make an informed decision.

FINAL REFLECTION QUESTIONS

As a final discussion, consider the following:

- What excites you the most about this option?

- What hesitations are you experiencing?

- How does this option differ from others you are considering?

HOW TO DETERMINE IF A GAP SEASON IS A GOOD FIT FOR YOU

 FOUNDATION QUESTIONS

- What most appeals to you about the idea of a gap season?

- How did you arrive at this opinion?

- What ideas do you currently have about how you will spend your time during this season?

- What benefits do you believe a gap season could provide for your future career ideas?

- What drawbacks do you think this option would have for your future career?

💼 EXPLORATORY QUESTIONS

If your teen struggles to identify a particular gap season plan you can discuss the following questions:

- What do you hope will happen personally for you as the result of a gap season?

- What do you hope will happen professionally for you as the result of a gap season?

- What activities are you interested in that a different option may not be able to give you?

- How long do you anticipate/want your gap season to last?

- What do you hope to be able to do after your gap season has concluded?

- How will your gap season plan help you achieve your career goals?

RESEARCH QUESTIONS

What research have you done to discover gap season opportunities?

If a teen has not done any research, here are a few places to have them start:

- Gap Year Association: https://gapyearassociation.org/gap-year.php

- EF Gap Year: https://efgapyear.com/gap-year-program/

- The Best Gap Year Programs of 2019-2020 (article): https://www.goabroad.com/articles/gap-year/best-gap-year-programs

- Gap Force: https://gapforce.org/us

 ## FUTURE IMPLICATIONS QUESTIONS

The following general questions can help your teen create a solid plan for a gap season:

- When do you want your gap season to begin?

- What goals do you hope to achieve by having a gap season?

- What organization(s) are you most interested in working with during your gap season?

- How will these organizations help you with your goals?

- What timeline do you need to develop to bring your plan to life?

- What budget do you need to set to make your plan a reality?

- How will you earn this money?

- How can we support you during your gap season?

 FINAL REFLECTION QUESTIONS

As a final discussion, consider the following:

- What excites you the most about this option?

- What hesitations are you experiencing?

- How does this option differ from others you are considering?

HOW TO DETERMINE IF A 4-YEAR COLLEGE IS A GOOD FIT FOR YOU

FOUNDATION QUESTIONS

- What most appeals to you about attending a 4-year college after high school?

- How did you arrive at this opinion?

- What benefits do you believe a 4-year college could provide for your future career ideas?

- What drawbacks do you think this option would have for your future career?

EXPLORATORY QUESTIONS

- What school(s) are you most interested in?

- What about this school/these schools appeals to you?

- What major(s) are you considering?

- If your teen has no idea:

  - Review the discussion questions from the first part of this Next Steps Guide to determine a particular career cluster area.

  - Using that career cluster area, have your teen research potential careers and the degrees and experience required (if necessary) for those careers.

  - Have your teen make a list of potential majors associated with the required degrees.

- What career(s) do you hope a degree in this area will lead to?

 RESEARCH QUESTIONS

Have your teen look up each college they are interested in and answer the following questions:

- What majors and minors are offered by this college that can lead to a career in the career cluster you are interested in?

- What is the average length of time to achieve the needed degree at this school?

- What is the job placement rate for graduates of this school?

- What internship opportunities does this school provide?

- What does it cost to go to this school for the length of time you will need to earn your degree?

  ○ Tuition costs

  ○ Books/supplies/fees costs

  ○ Room and board costs (residence halls and apartment living)

  ○ Transportation costs

  ○ In-state tuition vs out-of-state tuition (if considering an out-of-state school, note how residency can be gained)

- How does this cost compare to what would be spent on general education units at a community college? (This may be especially helpful information for those seeking to attend an out-of-state school and need to establish residency.)

- What do you think about that cost difference?

FUTURE IMPLICATIONS QUESTIONS

In considering the costs of college there are several questions to reflect upon:

- How do you plan to pay for your education?

    ○ Parents: what part of your student's college education will you fund (if any, as this is not a requirement) and what they will have to fund is an important conversation.

- What is the average starting salary for the careers you are interested in?

- Will you have to take out loans to pay for this school?

- How would you rate the return on your investment in your future by attending this school?

- Will your student debt be able to be paid off by your career?

- How long will it take?

  ○ Consider researching student loan rates. The StudentAid.gov site (https://student-aid.gov/understand-aid/types/loans/interest-rates) lists the most up-to-date government loan rates. Also, check out your local banks for their rates and compare them.

  ○ Add your potential loan amount, interest rate, and length of time desired to pay it off into a debt calculator like this one from BankRate.com: https://www.bank-rate.com/calculators/college-planning/loan-calculator.aspx

 FINAL REFLECTION QUESTIONS

As a final discussion, consider the following:

- What excites you the most about this option?

- What hesitations are you experiencing?

- How does this option differ from others you are considering?

FOR PARENTS

If you are funding all or part of your student's education, what boundaries do you need to establish for your student?

- Will you expect GPA minimums to remain in school?

- What happens if they fail a required class?

- If they are placed on academic probation, what will be your response?

- Will you financially reward your student for grades?

- Will you be paying for housing and personal expenses?

- Will you pay for participation in Greek Life if your teen chooses to pursue a sorority or fraternity?

HOW TO DETERMINE IF A COLLEGIATE ATHLETE IS A GOOD FIT FOR YOU

FOUNDATION QUESTIONS

- What most appeals to you about the idea of playing collegiate sports?

- What level do you want to play (D1, D2, etc.)?

- What about this level most appeals to you?

- Would you consider other levels? What would be the determining factor(s) for you to choose a different/additional level?

EXPLORATORY QUESTIONS

- What are your plans for this sport after college?

- What future career are you currently imagining for yourself?

- How will playing sports at the collegiate level help you with this future?

- How could it negatively impact your education?

RESEARCH QUESTIONS

- What research have you done to discover what schools you might be able to play for?

If your teen has not done any research, consider having them complete the following:

- Have your teenager research the various levels of play and search for a list of schools within the level(s) they want to play for. The NCAA has a comprehensive search tool on their website: http://www.ncaa.org/about/who-we-are/search-school

- Have your student narrow down their potential list of schools by

    ◦ level of play

    ◦ geographic location

    ◦ major they are interested in

    ◦ how long it will take to graduate

    ◦ tuition costs

    ◦ application requirements

    ◦ attendance costs (including room and board)

Note: you may want to complete the questions for the 4-year college option at the same time.

👟 RECRUITING PREPARATION QUESTIONS

Once your teen has this information, have them determine what schools they may be eligible to play for from their list based on their academics.

- Even with a formal offer from a coach, if your teenager does not meet the minimum application requirements, they will not be admitted to the school.

- Discuss with your teen what it will take financially for them to attend each school they are interested in, including any financial assistance you may be providing.

- Discuss with your teen what it will take for them to be successful at each school they are interested in.

- Once your teen has a solid list of schools they want to pursue, have them research the teams for each school they are interested in.

- Once your teen has a solid list of prospective schools, have them share their list with their current coach and discuss how to move forward in the recruiting process.

FINAL REFLECTION QUESTIONS

As a final discussion, consider the following:

- What excites you the most about this option?

- What hesitations are you experiencing?

- How does this option differ from others you are considering?

 FOR PARENTS

Note: The recruiting process is complex. Please consider having your teen discuss their thoughts with their coach(es) and take the time to explore the NCAA website: NCAA.org.

ENDNOTES

[1] Sometimes referred to as IGP's, these meetings are held yearly between counselors and students to determine which classes to take based on what they want to do after high school.

[2] Flannery, Mary Ellen. "The Epidemic of Anxiety Among Today's Students". *National Education Association*, Published March 28, 2018, Updated March 2019, https://www.nea.org/advocating-for-change/new-from-nea/epidemic-anxiety-among-todays-students

[3] Buffini, Brian. "The 5 C's of Young Achievers." The Brian Buffini Show, episode 244, September 29, 2020, https://www.thebrianbuffinishow.com/the-5-cs-of-young-achievers-244/

[4] Issa, Natalie. "U.S. Average Student Loan Debt Statistics." *Credit.Com*, June 19, 2019, https://www.credit.com/personal-finance/average-student-loan-debt/

[5] "The Advantages of Attending a Trade School". *HVAC Technical Institute*, October 16, 2014, https://www.hvac-tech.com/the-advantages-of-attending-a-trade-school/

[6] Posts, Legacy. "The Benefits of Trade Schools". *STEM Jobs Career Network*, April 27, 2016, https://edu.stemjobs.com/benefits-trade-schools/

[7] Stowasser, Melissa J, Assistant Vice President of Community Partnerships at Trident Technical College. Personal Interview. 5 November 2020.

[8] Information about the IFA Group can be found here: https://ifa-group.com/en/

[9] Vail, Chad, Work-based Learning Partnerships Coordinator for Charleston County School District. Personal Interview. 31 December 2020

[10] Parker, Kim; Cilluffo, Anthony; and Stepler, Renee. "6 facts about the U.S. military and its changing demographics". *Pew Research Center*, April 13, 2017, https://www.pew research.org/fact-tank/2017/04/13/6-facts-about-the-u-s-military-and-its-changingdemographics/

[11] Lewis, Robin, US Naval Captain. Personal Interview. 6 October 2020 and 20 October 2020.

[12] Muse, Kristi. "Understanding Post 9/11 GI Bill Benefits – Eligibility, Payment Rates, Monthly Housing Allowance, and More". TheMilitaryWallet.com, April 19, 2020, https://the militarywallet.com/post-9-11-gi-bill/

[13] Guest Writer. "Should I Join the Military? 11 Reasons the Military is a Good Career Option". *TheMilitaryWallet.com*, April 10, 2019, https://themilitarywallet.com/reasons-to-join-the-military/

[14] "Join the Military". *USA.gov*, https://www.usa.gov/join-military

[15] Guest Writer. "Should I Join the Military? 11 Reasons the Military is a Good Career Option". *The Military Wallet.com*, April 10, 2019, https://themilitarywallet.com/reasons-to-join-the-military/

[16] Powers, Rod. "Enlisting in the Army a Step-By-Step Guide". *TheBalanceCareers.com*, updated November 20, 2019, https://www.the-balancecareers.com/enlisting-in-the-army-step-by-step-3344830

[17] Moody, Josh. "What ROTC Programs Are and How They Work." *USNews.com*, Aug. 12, 2020, https://www.usnews.com/education/best-colleges/what-rotc-programs-are-and-how-they-work

18 Moon, Kristen. "What Students Need to Know Before Applying to One of The United States Military Academies". *Forbes.com*, August 20, 2019, https://www.forbes.com/sites/kristenmoon/2019/08/20/what-students-need-to-know-before-applying-to-one-of-the-united-states-military-academies/#50ca0a70348c

19 "What is a Gap Year?". *GapYearAssociation.org*, https://gapyearassociation.org/gap-year.php

20 Bahney, Anna. "College grads earn $30,000 a year more than people with just a high school degree". *CNN Business*, June 6, 2019, https://www.cnn.com/2019/06/06/success/college-worth-it/index.html

21 Bustamante, Jaleesa. "Average Cost of College & Tuition". *EducationData.org*, June 7, 2019, https://educationdata.org/average-cost-of-college/

22 Student-Athletes/Future/Want to Play College Sports? *National Collegiate Athletics Association*, http://www.ncaa.org/student-athletes/future

23 "College Recruiting Process: How Do Colleges Recruit Athletes?". *Next College Student Athlete*, https://www.ncsasports.org/recruiting/how-to-get-recruited/college-recruiting-process#top

24 Ciotti, Gregory. "The Most Important Mindset for Long-term Success". *The Sparring Mind*, https://www.sparringmind.com/growth-mindset/

25 Leaf, Caroline. *Think Learn Succeed*. Grand Rapids, MI, Baker Books, 2018.